I Dream, I Dare, I Do!

Dedication

This book is dedicated to the dreamers, the daredevils, and the doers – to everyone who has ever felt the whisper of a dream, the sting of self-doubt, and the exhilarating rush of taking a leap of faith. It is dedicated to those who stumble and rise again, persevere through challenges, and never give up on pursuing their passions. This is for the individuals who embrace the journey, finding fulfillment not just in the destination, but in the transformative power of the process itself. It is for those who dare to be different, refuse to settle for mediocrity, and strive to live a life aligned with their deepest values and aspirations. To the quiet revolutionaries changing the world one dream at a time, this book is a testament to your unwavering spirit and indomitable will. To the brave hearts who chase their wildest dreams with relentless passion and unwavering belief in themselves, this book is your compass, guide, and unwavering support system on the incredible journey of self-discovery and personal fulfillment. To you, the courageous souls who choose to dream big, dare greatly, and then do the work – this book is for you. May it serve as a constant reminder of your inherent strength, resilience, and limitless potential. May it inspire you to continue to chase your dreams with unwavering determination, to overcome every obstacle with grace and resilience, and to live a life of purpose and profound meaning.

Preface

The seed of this book was planted in countless conversations with individuals from all walks of life – young adults navigating uncertain career paths, established professionals seeking a renewed sense of purpose, and those facing significant life transitions or challenges. What I consistently heard was a yearning for something more, a desire to break free from limitations, both self-imposed and external. People felt stuck, unsure of how to translate their dreams into tangible reality. They yearned for a practical roadmap, a beacon of hope to guide them through the labyrinth of selfdoubt and fear. "I Dream, I Dare, I Do!" is the culmination of those conversations, born from a deep understanding of the struggles and aspirations of others, and a commitment to empowering them to achieve their full potential. This book isn't just a collection of theoretical concepts; it's a blend of practical strategies, inspirational stories, and motivational exercises designed to help you unearth your inner compass, embrace the courage to dare, and take the decisive action needed to transform your dreams into a reality. It is a testament to the power of human potential, a celebration of the incredible journey of self-discovery, and a guide to help you unlock your own unique greatness. It is my hope that the pages that follow will serve as a catalyst for transformation, empowering you to build unshakeable confidence, overcome your deepest fears, and create a life of purpose and fulfillment. Remember, the journey of a thousand miles begins with a single step. Let this book be the springboard that launches you on your extraordinary adventure.

Introduction

We all have dreams. Those whispers of possibility, the fleeting visions of a brighter future, the deep-seated desires that reside within our hearts. But for many, those dreams remain just that – dreams. They remain trapped in the confines of our imaginations, held back by fear, self-doubt, and a perceived lack of ability. This book is your invitation to break free from those limitations, to shed the shackles of self-doubt and embrace the exhilarating power of possibility. "I Dream, I Dare, I Do!" is a practical guide designed to empower you to pursue your aspirations with unwavering confidence and relentless determination. Structured around three core themes – Dream, Dare, and Do – it provides a clear roadmap for personal growth and achievement. The first part, "Dream," will guide you on a journey of selfdiscovery, helping you identify your true passions and translate your vague aspirations into concrete, achievable goals. You'll learn how to visualize success, overcome limiting beliefs, and craft a personal mission statement that will act as your guiding star on this incredible journey. The second part, "Dare," tackles the fear and self-doubt that often hold us back. Through powerful storytelling and actionable strategies, you'll learn how to step outside your comfort zone, build resilience, and cultivate unwavering self-belief. The final part, "Do," emphasizes the importance of action. You'll discover practical tips and techniques to turn your aspirations into tangible reality, building momentum, managing setbacks, and staying motivated on your path to success. This book is more than just a self-help guide; it's a companion on your journey, a source of inspiration, and a toolkit to help you navigate the challenges and celebrate the triumphs along the way. Get ready to embark on an incredible adventure of self-discovery. Get ready to dream big, dare greatly, and do the work. Get ready to live the life you've always envisioned.

Recognizing Your Passions

The journey to fulfilling your dreams begins with a profound understanding of yourself – a journey inward to discover the compass that guides your life. This isn't about finding a prepackaged, societal definition of success; it's about unearthing your *own* True North, the passions that burn bright within your soul. This inner compass points towards your authentic self, the desires that resonate deeply and consistently, fueling your spirit with an unwavering energy. Finding this internal GPS requires introspection, a willingness to delve into the recesses of your mind and heart, to uncover the hidden treasures buried beneath layers of routine and expectation.

Imagine your life as a vast, unexplored landscape. You've perhaps walked along familiar paths, the well-trodden routes of habit and obligation. But what lies beyond those familiar trails? What breathtaking vistas, hidden waterfalls, and majestic peaks await your discovery? Your passions are the maps to these undiscovered territories, the keys to unlocking a life filled with purpose and joy.

One of the most effective tools for this exploration is journaling. Find a quiet space, free from distractions, where you can connect with your inner voice. Grab a notebook and pen – the simple act of writing by hand often fosters a deeper connection to your thoughts and emotions than typing on a keyboard. Begin by simply writing whatever comes to mind. Don't censor yourself; let your thoughts flow freely, unburdened by judgment or self-criticism. This isn't about producing a polished piece of writing; it's about releasing the thoughts and feelings that may be blocking your path to selfdiscovery.

Ask yourself powerful questions. What activities have brought me genuine joy and fulfillment in the past? What tasks do I lose myself in, forgetting the passage of time? What did I dream of doing as a child, before societal expectations and self-doubt began to creep in? Reflect on moments of profound happiness. What circumstances, people, or activities contributed to those feelings? These moments are not mere coincidences; they are clues, breadcrumbs leading you towards your true desires.

Mindful reflection is another crucial element of this process. Take time each day to pause, breathe deeply, and simply observe your thoughts and feelings without judgment. Notice the sensations in your body, the rhythm of your breath. Cultivate a sense of awareness of your inner world, paying attention to the subtle cues that your passions may be sending you. Are you consistently drawn to certain topics or activities? Do you experience a surge of energy or excitement when engaging in particular pursuits? These are often subtle indicators of your True North.

Consider your past successes. What achievements are you most proud of? What skills or talents do you possess that bring you a sense of accomplishment? These past triumphs often hold valuable insights into your natural strengths and inclinations. They provide a foundation upon which you can build your future endeavors. Remember, identifying your passions is not about seeking perfection; it's about recognizing the things that ignite your spirit and bring you a sense of purpose.

Take some time to examine your current life. Are you feeling fulfilled? If not, what's missing? This honest self-assessment is a crucial step in aligning your actions with your passions. Don't be afraid to acknowledge feelings of dissatisfaction or unfulfillment. These are important indicators that something needs to change, a sign that you may be drifting away from your True North.

Don't underestimate the power of small, seemingly insignificant moments. Perhaps it's the feeling of satisfaction you get from baking bread, the joy of nurturing a garden, or the thrill of solving a complex problem. These seemingly small pleasures often hold the key to uncovering your deeper passions. They are whispers from your soul, guiding you towards a life of greater meaning and purpose. Pay attention to those whispers. They often hold the most profound insights into your authentic self.

This process isn't a race. It's a journey of self-discovery, a gradual unveiling of your authentic self. Be patient with yourself. Allow yourself the space and time to explore your thoughts and feelings without judgment. The more you engage in this process of introspection, the clearer your vision will become, the brighter your inner compass will shine, guiding you towards a life lived with purpose, passion, and unwavering joy. Embrace this journey of self-discovery. The rewards that await are immeasurable. The fulfillment that comes from aligning your actions with your passions is a gift you'll carry with you for a lifetime.

Remember, discovering your passions isn't just about identifying your hobbies. It's about understanding what truly motivates you, what makes you feel alive, and what leaves you feeling profoundly fulfilled. It's about uncovering the core values that underpin your being and aligning your choices with those values. This is about identifying the unique blend of talents, interests, and values that makes you, you.

Take time to reflect on past experiences where you felt intensely engaged and energized. What was it about those experiences that captivated you? Was it the creative process, the challenge, the collaborative effort, or the opportunity to make a difference? Identifying these underlying drivers is key to understanding your passions. These insights will help you discern between activities that are simply time-fillers and those that genuinely resonate with your soul.

Once you've identified some potential passions, it's important to consider the practical implications. Are these passions something you can realistically pursue? Do you have the skills and resources needed to cultivate these passions? If not, how can you acquire them? This isn't about abandoning your aspirations, but about developing a realistic plan for achieving your goals.

Don't be discouraged if your passions seem initially overwhelming or unattainable. Break them down into smaller, manageable steps. Create a roadmap for yourself, outlining the skills you need to develop, the resources you require, and the steps you will take to turn your passions into reality. Remember, even the most ambitious goals can be achieved through consistent effort and a clear plan of action.

Finally, remember that discovering your passions is an ongoing journey, not a destination. Your interests and values may evolve over time. Be open to new experiences and willing to adapt your path as you learn and grow. The key is to remain curious, receptive, and committed to the process of self-discovery. Your True North may shift over time, and that is perfectly okay. Embrace the journey, and allow your passions to guide you towards a life of purpose and joy. Your passions are not merely hobbies; they are the compass that guides you towards a life authentically your own.

Defining Your Aspirations

We've embarked on a journey of self-discovery, unearthing the whispers of your inner compass, those passions that hum beneath the surface of everyday life. But knowing what ignites your soul is only the first step. The path from a vague yearning to a tangible reality requires a crucial transition: transforming those hazy aspirations into vivid, achievable goals. Think of it as moving from a blurry photograph to a sharp, high-definition image – the details suddenly become clear, the path forward becomes illuminated.

This is where the power of SMART goals comes in. You might have heard the acronym before: Specific, Measurable, Achievable, Relevant, and Time-Bound. It's more than just a catchy phrase; it's a framework for transforming dreams into concrete plans. Let's break down each element:

Specificity: Vague dreams are like shooting arrows in the dark. "I want to be successful" is a wish, not a goal. Success, in this instance, lacks specificity. Success *in what area*? What does success *look like* for you? A specific goal might be: "I want to write and publish a novel within the next two years." Notice the clarity? It focuses on a particular outcome, a specific action – writing and publishing a novel.

Let's consider another example. "I want to be healthier" is an aspiration, not a concrete goal. A more specific goal could be: "I want to lose 15 pounds and run a 5k race in six months." See how much more focused and measurable this goal is?

Now, let's explore your own aspirations. Take a moment to write down three of your most significant dreams – the ones that tug at your heartstrings and fill you with a sense of purpose. Don't censor yourself; let the words flow freely. Once you've listed them, let's refine them, turning them into specific, actionable goals.

Measurability: How will you know if you've achieved your goal? This is where measurability comes into play. Your goal needs quantifiable metrics, something you can track and measure your progress against. Returning to the novel example, you might track your progress by setting weekly word count goals, or by completing specific chapters by certain deadlines. For the health goal, the weight loss and the 5k race are measurable objectives.

Think about your own aspirations. How will you know you've achieved them? What milestones can you set along the way? For each of your three goals, write down how you'll measure your progress. Will it be through a number of completed tasks, a specific amount of weight lost, a certain amount of money saved, or perhaps the achievement of a specific skill?

Achievability: Ambitious goals are fantastic, but they must be realistic within the context of your resources and time frame. Setting unattainable goals can lead to frustration and discouragement. While it's important to push your boundaries, it's equally important to make sure the goal you set is realistically achievable given your resources, capabilities, and the time available. Achievability doesn't mean settling for less; it means being strategic and pragmatic in your approach.

Consider your current skills, resources, and time constraints. Are your goals aligned with your capabilities? If not, what steps can you take to bridge the gap? Perhaps you need to acquire new skills, gather additional resources, or adjust your timeline. For instance, if your goal is to run a marathon in six months with zero prior experience, you need a more realistic training plan to break that goal into smaller, achievable increments.

Relevance: Your goals must be aligned with your values, your long-term vision, and your overall sense of purpose. Chasing goals that don't resonate with your core values can lead to a sense of emptiness, even if you achieve them. A goal may be specific, measurable, and achievable, but if it's not relevant to your life's overall direction, it simply won't hold the same weight or meaning. Ask yourself if each of your goals aligns with your larger aspirations and the person you want to become.

Review your three goals again. Do they resonate deeply with who you are and where you envision yourself in the future?
If not, reconsider your approach and refine your goals. Consider adjusting the timeframe if necessary. Sometimes, the importance of a goal can justify a longer-term commitment.

Time-Bound: Deadlines provide structure and motivation. They create a sense of urgency and accountability, preventing procrastination. A time-bound goal has a clear start and end date, which is crucial to creating a plan to achieve the goal. Specificity doesn't necessarily require a timeline, but a time-bound goal is a concrete step to achieve a goal and it holds you accountable.

For each of your three goals, set a realistic deadline. Breaking down large goals into smaller, manageable steps with deadlines for each is crucial for maintaining momentum. For instance, if your goal is to write a novel in two years, break it down into quarterly milestones, such as completing a specific number of chapters or reaching a certain word count. For your health goal, create a weekly workout schedule with specific targets. The clearer and more precise your timeline, the better you'll be able to track your progress and stay motivated.

Breaking Down the Mountain: Large, ambitious goals can often seem overwhelming. The key to overcoming this feeling is to break them down into smaller, more manageable steps. Think of it as tackling a mountain one manageable step at a time, instead of trying to scale the entire peak in one leap. Each small step contributes to the bigger picture, building momentum and confidence. Celebrate each small victory along the way, which will reinforce your motivation and commitment. Rewarding yourself after completing each milestone boosts your morale and keeps you moving forward.

Let's illustrate this with the novel-writing goal. Instead of focusing on the entire novel at once, break it down into manageable chunks: outlining the plot, writing a chapter a week, editing each chapter, and finding a literary agent or publisher. Each of these sub-goals has its own smaller, timebound objectives. Similarly, the health goal can be broken down into weekly workout routines, a tailored dietary plan, and regular check-ins to monitor your progress.

Now, take another look at your three goals. Break each one down into smaller, actionable steps. Assign deadlines to each step, making them specific, measurable, and achievable within your available time and resources. This process transforms your overwhelming aspirations into a series of manageable tasks, making the journey toward your dreams feel less daunting and more exciting.

Remember, the journey from vague visions to vivid goals is a process. It requires introspection, planning, and a willingness to adjust your course as needed. But with clarity, commitment, and a well-defined plan, you will transform your dreams from distant possibilities into tangible realities, one step at a time. Embrace the journey, celebrate the small victories, and remember that the power to shape your future lies within your grasp. You've already taken the first brave step by identifying your inner compass; now, it's time to chart your course towards a future that reflects your truest aspirations.

Painting a Picture of Success

We've identified the whispers of your heart, the dreams that flicker like fireflies on a summer night. We've brought those flickering lights into sharper focus, transforming vague aspirations into concrete goals. But even the clearest goal remains a distant shore without a map, a compass, and a powerful engine to propel you forward. That engine, my friends, is the power of visualization.

Visualization isn't just about passively imagining your success; it's about actively creating a sensory experience, a vivid mental movie of your triumphant future. It's about engaging all your senses – sight, sound, smell, taste, and touch – to paint a picture so real, so vibrant, that it feels as tangible as holding your dream in your hands.

Think of your goal – perhaps it's finishing a marathon, writing a novel, starting a business, or mastering a musical instrument. Now, close your eyes. Don't just think about crossing the finish line, feel the pounding of your heart, the burn in your lungs, the exhilaration as you break through the tape. Hear the cheers of the crowd, the announcer's voice booming your name. Smell the fresh air, taste the sweat on your lips, feel the medal cold and heavy around your neck. Engage all your senses, creating a three-dimensional experience that transports you to that moment of victory.

This isn't mere daydreaming; it's strategic mental rehearsal. Athletes use this technique to hone their skills and build mental resilience. Entrepreneurs use it to envision successful business strategies and overcome obstacles. Artists use it to create masterpieces. The power of visualization lies in its ability to rewire your brain, forging new neural pathways that connect your dreams to your actions.

Imagine yourself writing that novel. Feel the weight of the manuscript in your hands, the satisfying click of the keyboard, the flow of words onto the page. See the cover design, vibrant and captivating. Hear the praise from readers, the positive reviews glowing online. Smell the fresh ink of the printed book. Taste the celebratory champagne at your book launch.

Or perhaps your dream is to start a business. Visualize your office, buzzing with activity. See your team working collaboratively, sharing ideas and celebrating successes. Hear the ring of the cash register, the excited voices of satisfied customers. Smell the fresh coffee brewing in the breakroom, taste the cake at your company's anniversary celebration, feel the weight of responsibility and the immense satisfaction of building something from the ground up.

The key is to make your visualizations as detailed and multisensory as possible. The more vivid and engaging your mental picture, the more powerful its influence on your subconscious mind. This isn't about escaping reality; it's about creating a powerful blueprint for your future, a roadmap guiding you toward your goals.

However, visualization is not simply about the grand finale. It's about visualizing the entire journey, the challenges you'll face, and the strategies you'll employ to overcome them. Anticipating obstacles allows you to develop solutions beforehand, building resilience and confidence. Imagine encountering a setback – maybe a crucial funding source falls through for your business, or you face a critical writer's block. Don't just visualize the problem; visualize yourself finding a solution, adapting your strategy, overcoming the obstacle, learning from the experience, and emerging stronger.

This process of visualizing challenges and solutions builds mental fortitude. It's about building resilience, preparing yourself for the inevitable bumps in the road. It's about seeing the potential hurdles not as insurmountable obstacles, but as opportunities for growth and learning. This is where visualization truly transforms from a simple exercise into a powerful tool for self-mastery.

Furthermore, don't just focus on the external manifestations of success. Visualize the inner transformation that accompanies achieving your goals. Imagine the sense of accomplishment, the boost in self-confidence, the increased self-belief. Feel the pride in yourself, not just for achieving your goal, but for the journey you undertook to get there.

This inner transformation is often the most profound and lasting reward. The feeling of accomplishment, the satisfaction of overcoming challenges, the growth in selfesteem—these are the true measures of success. Visualizing these feelings, these internal shifts, strengthens your commitment and fuels your perseverance. It allows you to connect to the deeper motivations driving your dreams, reinforcing your commitment to the process.

Another important aspect of visualization is consistency. Just like any other skill, it requires regular practice. Set aside a few minutes each day to engage in your visualization exercises. Make it a ritual, a sacred space where you connect with your dreams and nurture your aspirations. The more consistently you engage in this practice, the stronger the neural pathways will become, and the more effectively your subconscious mind will work to guide you towards your goals.

Consider using visual aids to enhance your visualization practice. Create a vision board with images and quotes that represent your goals. Surround yourself with objects and symbols that inspire you. Listen to music that evokes feelings of motivation and accomplishment. These external cues will reinforce your mental images and deepen the impact of your visualization sessions.

Remember, visualization is not a magical shortcut; it's a powerful tool to enhance your focus, build your confidence, and strengthen your resolve. It's about aligning your mind and body with your aspirations, creating a potent synergy that propels you forward. It's about creating a compelling narrative of your future, a story you are actively writing, one visualization at a time.

It's also crucial to remember that visualization isn't about wishful thinking. It's a complement to action, not a replacement for it. Visualization provides the mental fuel; action provides the physical momentum. The two work hand in hand, creating a powerful force that propels you toward your dreams. Visualizing success is like designing a blueprint; taking action is like building the house. Both are essential for achieving your desired outcome.

Don't be discouraged if you find it challenging at first. Like any skill, visualization requires practice and patience. Start with small, achievable goals and gradually increase the complexity of your visualizations. Be kind to yourself, and celebrate your progress along the way. Remember, the journey itself is a significant part of the process. The more you practice, the more vivid and effective your visualizations will become.

Finally, remember the importance of belief. Believe in your ability to achieve your goals. Believe in the power of visualization to guide and support you. Believe in yourself. This unwavering belief, combined with consistent visualization, will create a powerful force that propels you toward success. Your dreams are not just fantasies; they are blueprints for your future. Now, it's time to paint them in vivid detail, and watch them come to life. Believe in the power of your own imagination, the potency of your own dreams, and the strength of your own will. You are capable of achieving extraordinary things; now, let's make those dreams a reality. The journey may be long, but with every step, with every visualization, you are getting closer to the life you've always imagined. The power is within you; now unleash it.

Reframing Negative SelfTalk

The journey to realizing your dreams isn't solely paved with sunshine and rainbows. Obstacles will arise, detours will appear, and sometimes, the most formidable opponent you'll face resides within: your own mind. We've glimpsed the radiant potential within, we've visualized the vibrant tapestry of your future, but now we must confront the insidious whispers of self-doubt, the limiting beliefs that hold you captive in a cage of your own making. These are the internal saboteurs, the insidious voices that tell you "you're not good enough," "you'll fail," or "it's too late." These aren't external forces; they are internal narratives, selfimposed limitations that prevent you from reaching your full potential.

Think of these limiting beliefs as weeds choking the vibrant flowers of your aspirations. They sprout from the fertile ground of past experiences, insecurities, and negative selftalk. Perhaps you've faced setbacks in the past, experiences that have left deep emotional scars, leading you to believe you are incapable of achieving your dreams. Maybe you've internalized criticism from others, allowing their doubts to overshadow your own potential. These beliefs, while seemingly innocuous, are powerful forces that can derail your progress before you even begin. They are the insidious seeds of fear, disguised as rational thought, whispering lies of inadequacy.

But here's the liberating truth: these beliefs are not immutable. They are not facts etched in stone. They are merely interpretations, stories we tell ourselves, narratives we can rewrite. Just as a gardener diligently weeds their garden, cultivating healthy growth, you can consciously cultivate a positive mindset, uprooting the negativity and planting seeds of self-belief and empowerment. The process of conquering these limiting beliefs is a journey of selfdiscovery, a powerful act of reclaiming your narrative and shaping your destiny.

Let's begin with identifying these insidious beliefs. Take a moment, close your eyes, and delve into the depths of your mind. What are the recurring negative thoughts that plague you? What are the self-limiting beliefs that hold you back? Write them down. Don't censor yourself. Let everything flow freely onto the page. This isn't a judgment exercise; it's a process of honest self-reflection. This is about acknowledging the enemy, understanding its tactics, before we can effectively combat it.

Once you've identified your limiting beliefs, the next step is to challenge their validity. Ask yourself: Is this belief truly accurate? Is there evidence to support this belief, or is it based on fear, assumptions, or past experiences that may no longer be relevant? Often, these beliefs are rooted in fear of failure, fear of judgment, or fear of the unknown. They are based on hypothetical scenarios, 'what ifs' that often never materialize.

For example, let's say you harbor the belief, "I'm not creative enough to write a novel." Challenge this belief. Have you ever tried writing? What evidence supports this claim? Perhaps you haven't tried writing, or you attempted a short story and felt it wasn't up to par. But that doesn't mean you lack creativity. It simply means you haven't yet explored your creative potential fully. Consider the countless successful authors who started with humble beginnings, who initially doubted their abilities but persisted, honing their craft with every attempt. Their stories are testaments to the power of perseverance and belief in oneself.

Another common limiting belief is, "I'm too old to start something new." Age is merely a number. Consider the many inspiring stories of individuals who embarked on new adventures later in life, achieving remarkable success against all odds. Their success is a testament to the fact that age is not a barrier but a testament to resilience and experience. It's never too late to pursue your dreams. The past does not dictate your future; you do.

Now, let's take those limiting beliefs and actively reframe them into empowering affirmations. This is where we transform negative self-talk into positive reinforcement. If your limiting belief is, "I'm not good enough," reframe it as, "I am capable, and I am constantly growing and learning." If your belief is, "I'll fail," reframe it as, "I will learn from my mistakes and use them to propel me forward." If you believe
"It's too late," reframe it to "It's the perfect time to start."

This reframing process isn't about ignoring the negative; it's about acknowledging it and then consciously choosing a more empowering perspective. It's about replacing selfcriticism with self-compassion, self-doubt with self-belief. Think of it as a mental detox, cleansing your mind of negativity and replacing it with positivity. It takes conscious effort and consistent practice, but the rewards are immeasurable.

To further solidify this process, incorporate daily affirmations into your routine. Write down your positive affirmations and repeat them to yourself several times a day. Speak them aloud, feeling the power of the words resonate within you. This conscious repetition reinforces the positive messages, subtly reprogramming your subconscious mind, gradually replacing the limiting beliefs with empowering affirmations. Imagine it as a gentle rain, nourishing the seeds of self-belief you've planted.

Consider using visualization in conjunction with your affirmations. Imagine yourself already achieving your goals. See yourself succeeding, feeling the sense of accomplishment and joy. Let your imagination paint a vivid picture of your future success. Combine the power of positive affirmations with the vividness of your visualizations, creating a powerful synergy to reinforce your belief in yourself and your ability to achieve your goals.

Remember, this is not a quick fix; it's a continuous process. There will be days when the negative whispers creep back, when self-doubt threatens to overshadow your progress. That's perfectly normal. Acknowledge those feelings without judgment, and gently redirect your thoughts back to your positive affirmations. The key is consistency and persistence. Keep nurturing your positive self-talk, keep visualizing your success, and keep taking those steps, however small, towards your dreams.

You are not defined by your past experiences or your past failures. You are not limited by what others may think or say. Your potential is limitless. You possess an inner strength and resilience that surpasses any obstacle. Embrace your power, believe in yourself, and let nothing hold you back from achieving the life you've always dreamed of. Your dreams are not just wishes; they are the blueprints of your future. Now, it's time to build them, brick by brick, with unwavering faith in your abilities and unwavering dedication to your goals. The journey is yours, the destination is waiting, and the power to achieve it rests entirely within you. Now go forth, and make your dreams a breathtaking reality. The world is waiting to see what you can accomplish. The only person standing in your way is you, and now you have the tools to conquer that obstacle. Believe in yourself, and the rest will follow. Remember, this is your journey, your life, your dreams. Dare to live them. Dare to become the best version of yourself. The world awaits.

Defining Your Purpose

Having unearthed the rich landscape of your dreams, having confronted and conquered the inner demons that sought to stifle your aspirations, we now arrive at a crucial juncture: crafting your personal mission statement. This isn't simply a catchy phrase; it's the cornerstone of your journey, the bedrock upon which you'll build your future, a guiding star in the sometimes-turbulent sea of life. It's a declaration of purpose, a concise yet powerful articulation of who you are, what you value, and where you're headed.

Think of your personal mission statement as your own unique North Star, constantly visible, providing unwavering direction even in the darkest of nights. It's a potent blend of your deepest values, your loftiest ambitions, and a clear vision of the impact you want to make on the world. Without it, you risk drifting aimlessly, pulled in various directions by fleeting desires and external pressures. With it, you possess a powerful tool to navigate the complexities of life and stay focused on what truly matters.

But how do you forge this essential instrument? How do you distill the essence of your dreams into a concise, inspiring statement? The process itself is a journey of self-discovery, a refinement of your understanding of yourself and your place in the world. It requires introspection, honesty, and a willingness to delve deep into your core values and aspirations.

Begin by asking yourself fundamental questions. What truly excites you? What ignites your passion and makes you feel alive? What unique talents and skills do you possess? These aren't superficial questions; they demand honest, soulsearching answers. Avoid the temptation to answer with what you *think* you should say or what others *expect* you to say. Tap into your authentic self, the core of your being, and let the answers flow freely from the wellspring of your true desires.

Consider the following prompts as a starting point:

What are my core values? What principles guide my decisions and shape my actions? Is it integrity, kindness, creativity, innovation, or something else entirely? List them all, no matter how seemingly insignificant. Each one contributes to the mosaic of who you are.

What are my biggest strengths? What skills and talents do I possess that set me apart? What do people consistently compliment me on? Identify these strengths not to boast, but to understand the unique contribution you can bring to the world.

What are my deepest desires? What legacy do I want to leave behind? What impact do I want to have on the world, however small or large? Don't limit your thinking; dream big. The world needs your unique perspective and contribution.

What are my long-term goals? Where do I see myself in five, ten, or twenty years? Paint a vivid picture of your future self, not just in terms of career or material possessions, but in terms of personal fulfillment and impact.

Once you've answered these questions honestly and thoroughly, you'll begin to see patterns emerge. You'll start to identify the recurring themes and values that underpin your dreams and aspirations. These are the building blocks of your personal mission statement.

Let's illustrate this with a few examples. Imagine Sarah, an aspiring artist who values creativity, self-expression, and social impact. After reflecting on her values and goals, her personal mission statement might be: "To create inspiring art that empowers and connects people, fostering a deeper
understanding and appreciation for the human experience."

Or consider David, a dedicated teacher who values knowledge, growth, and mentorship. His mission statement could be: "To inspire a lifelong love of learning in my students, empowering them to reach their full potential and
become responsible, compassionate global citizens."

And consider Maria, an entrepreneur who values innovation, sustainability, and social responsibility. Her statement might read: "To build a thriving and environmentally conscious business that creates opportunities for others while
contributing to a more sustainable future."

Notice how these statements are concise, inspiring, and action-oriented. They aren't vague pronouncements; they provide a clear sense of purpose and direction. They reflect the individuals' core values and aspirations, serving as a guiding light in their daily lives.

Your personal mission statement doesn't have to be perfect on the first try. It's a living document, constantly evolving as you grow and learn. Treat it as a work in progress, refining it as you gain new insights and experiences. The important thing is to start the process, to begin articulating your purpose and creating a roadmap for your life.

This is not just about setting goals; it's about connecting with your deeper self, understanding your purpose, and aligning your actions with your values. It's about creating a life that's meaningful and fulfilling, a life that leaves a positive mark on the world. It's about living a life of purpose, driven by your own internal compass, rather than being swayed by external forces.

Remember, your personal mission statement is not meant to confine you; it's designed to liberate you. It's a declaration of your intention, a powerful affirmation of your potential, and a constant reminder of the impact you're striving to create. It provides the framework for making choices aligned with your values and pursuing your goals with clarity and purpose.

The process of crafting your personal mission statement isn't just an intellectual exercise; it's a profound act of selfdiscovery. It's an opportunity to connect with your deepest values, clarify your aspirations, and create a vision for your life that inspires and motivates you. It's a powerful tool for self-reflection and self-improvement, empowering you to live a life that's both meaningful and fulfilling.

As you embark on this journey of self-discovery, allow yourself the time and space to reflect deeply. Don't rush the process; allow your insights to unfold organically. Engage in activities that foster introspection, such as journaling, meditation, or spending time in nature. These practices can help you tap into your intuition and connect with your inner wisdom.

Once you've drafted your personal mission statement, don't just let it sit on a page. Integrate it into your daily life. Use it as a guiding principle in your decision-making. Refer to it regularly to stay focused on your goals and remind yourself of your purpose. Share it with others if you feel comfortable doing so; it can be a powerful tool for accountability and support.

The creation of your personal mission statement is just the beginning of a lifelong journey. It's a continuous process of refinement and growth, reflecting your evolving values and aspirations. As you progress on your path, you might find yourself adjusting or refining your statement to better reflect your current stage of development. This is entirely normal and expected.

This process is intensely personal and unique to you. There's no right or wrong way to craft your personal mission statement. The most important thing is that it resonates with you on a deep level, that it feels authentic and true to your core values and aspirations. It's a testament to your selfawareness, your courage to dream, and your unwavering commitment to living a life of purpose. And that, my friends, is a journey worth embarking on. So, take your time, explore your inner landscape, and craft a mission statement that will guide you toward a life brimming with meaning, fulfillment, and success. Your future self will thank you for it. Now, go forth and create your masterpiece. Your life awaits.

Recognizing Its Root Causes

Fear. That chilling whisper in the back of your mind, the icy grip that constricts your chest, the phantom limb that holds you back from leaping into the unknown. It's a universal experience, a primal instinct designed to protect us from danger. But in the pursuit of our dreams, fear often becomes a formidable foe, a self-imposed barrier that prevents us from realizing our full potential. This isn't about banishing fear entirely—that's unrealistic and, frankly, undesirable. Fear, in its healthy form, is a warning system, a crucial survival mechanism. The challenge lies in understanding its nuances, differentiating between a genuine threat and a selfcreated illusion, and learning to manage its power so it doesn't paralyze you.

Think of fear as a complex tapestry, woven from various threads. Some threads are easily identifiable, stemming from tangible threats – a looming deadline, a challenging presentation, a significant financial risk. These are often rational fears, rooted in potential negative consequences. We can address these by careful planning, preparation, and risk mitigation strategies. But other threads are far more subtle, insidious, woven from the fabric of our past experiences, our beliefs, and our self-perception. These are the irrational fears, the ghosts of past traumas, the echoes of limiting beliefs that whisper doubts and insecurities.

Let's delve into the roots of these irrational fears. Consider, for instance, the fear of public speaking. For some, it's a simple matter of lacking confidence or practice. They can overcome this with preparation and rehearsal. But for others, this fear might stem from a childhood experience – perhaps a humiliating moment in school, a critical parent, or a public embarrassment. The fear isn't just about the act of speaking, it's about the potential for repeating that past trauma, for reliving the feelings of vulnerability and shame. This is where we must unpack the emotional baggage.

Similarly, the fear of failure often masks deeper insecurities. It's not simply the fear of falling short of expectations; it's the fear of not being good enough, of being judged and rejected. This fear frequently originates from early childhood experiences, where we may have received conditional love, praise dependent on performance, or criticism that eroded our self-esteem. The fear of failure, in these cases, is a fear of losing the love or approval we crave. It's a fear that goes far beyond the immediate consequences of a setback.

Another common root of irrational fear is the fear of the unknown. This is often fueled by anxiety and a lack of control. We crave predictability and order, and the prospect of venturing into uncharted territory can feel overwhelming. This fear often stems from a need for security and a deepseated aversion to risk. This isn't necessarily a bad thing; risk aversion is a natural part of human nature. The challenge lies in learning to differentiate between calculated risks, where careful planning and preparation mitigate the potential for negative outcomes, and reckless actions that are truly dangerous.

Identifying the root causes of your fears is a crucial first step toward conquering them. This requires honest introspection, a willingness to confront your past, and a commitment to understanding your own emotional landscape. Journaling can be incredibly helpful in this process. Write down your fears, explore their origins, and identify any recurring patterns or themes. Don't shy away from difficult emotions; allow yourself to feel them, to understand them, and to process them. Talking to a therapist or counselor can also provide valuable insights and support. A skilled professional can help you unpack these emotional layers, address any underlying traumas, and develop coping mechanisms.

Remember that identifying the root cause isn't about assigning blame or dwelling on past hurts; it's about gaining self-awareness, understanding the mechanisms of your fear, and empowering yourself to take control. Once you understand the "why" behind your fears, you can begin to address them effectively. For example, if your fear of failure stems from a history of criticism, you can actively challenge those negative beliefs, focusing on self-compassion and celebrating your achievements, no matter how small. If your fear of the unknown is rooted in a need for control, you can learn to practice mindfulness, embrace uncertainty, and develop strategies for managing unpredictable situations.

Let's take the example of Sarah, a talented writer who dreams of publishing a novel but is paralyzed by the fear of rejection. She traced her fear back to a childhood experience where her creative writing in school was harshly criticized by a teacher. This criticism ingrained a belief that her work wasn't good enough, that she wasn't a good enough writer. This belief manifested itself as a crippling fear of rejection from publishers. Recognizing the root cause of her fear allowed Sarah to begin challenging this limiting belief. She started by focusing on the positive feedback she received from beta readers and focusing on the joy of the writing process itself rather than the outcome. This shift in perspective helped her to develop greater resilience and to approach the publishing process with renewed confidence.

Similarly, consider Mark, an entrepreneur who's hesitant to expand his business due to a fear of financial risk. His fear originated from witnessing his parents struggle financially when he was younger. This created a deep-seated aversion to debt and uncertainty. By understanding the roots of his fear, Mark began to develop a more sophisticated approach to financial planning. He created detailed budgets, sought expert advice, and meticulously assessed the risks and potential rewards of expansion. This careful planning reduced his anxiety significantly, enabling him to take measured steps towards growth.

Understanding the root causes of fear is not a quick fix; it's an ongoing process of self-discovery and self-acceptance. It requires courage, patience, and a commitment to selfcompassion. But by confronting your fears, by understanding their origins, and by developing effective coping mechanisms, you can transform them from paralyzing obstacles into stepping stones on your path to achieving your dreams. The journey may be challenging, but the rewards are immeasurable. Remember, embracing the courage to dare isn't about eliminating fear, it's about learning to dance with it, to harness its power, and to move forward despite its presence. The path to your dreams is paved with courage, and understanding your fears is the first step on that journey.

Embracing Calculated Risks

We've explored the shadowy realm of fear, dissected its origins, and begun to understand its insidious grip on our ambitions. Now, it's time to move beyond the analysis and into the arena of action. Confronting fear isn't just about understanding it; it's about actively choosing to step outside the familiar confines of your comfort zone. This isn't a reckless leap into the abyss, however. It's about embracing *calculated* risks – carefully considered steps that push your boundaries while minimizing unnecessary danger. Think of it as a meticulously planned expedition, not a blindfolded stumble.

The comfort zone, that cozy haven where routines reign supreme and uncertainty is banished, is often disguised as safety. But true growth, profound transformation, and the realization of your dreams rarely occur within those comfortable walls. Imagine a climber aiming for the summit of a formidable peak. They don't simply jump from base camp to the summit; they meticulously plan their ascent, setting incremental goals, establishing secure footholds, and assessing the risks at every stage. Your journey to achieving your dreams is much the same. It demands a strategic approach, a series of calculated risks designed to gradually expand your capabilities and confidence.

Consider a small, seemingly insignificant risk. Perhaps you've always dreamt of public speaking but the very thought sends shivers down your spine. Instead of aiming for a TED Talk on your first attempt, start small. Volunteer to share a brief anecdote at a team meeting, present a short report to a small group of colleagues, or join a local Toastmasters club. Each of these steps represents a calculated risk – a small foray outside your comfort zone that allows you to test your limits in a safe environment. The success of each small step builds momentum, fuels your confidence, and prepares you for progressively larger challenges.

This gradual approach is crucial. Trying to scale a mountain in a single, desperate leap is a recipe for disaster. Similarly, attempting to overcome your deepest fears with one grand, sweeping gesture is often counterproductive. It's more likely to result in failure and reinforce your fear, rather than conquering it. Remember the climber's methodical ascent – that's the key to successfully navigating the terrain of your fears.

Let's explore some practical strategies for taking calculated risks. First, identify your specific fears. What holds you back from pursuing your dreams? Is it the fear of failure, rejection, or public judgment? Once you pinpoint the specific fears, you can tailor your approach to address them head-on. For example, if you fear rejection, start by seeking feedback on your work from trusted sources. This gradually desensitizes you to criticism and builds resilience. If your fear is primarily related to public speaking, start with small presentations, as mentioned earlier, gradually increasing the size and formality of your audience.

Next, break down your larger goals into smaller, manageable steps. Instead of focusing on the daunting enormity of your aspirations, concentrate on the small, achievable steps that lead toward your ultimate objective. This approach helps to maintain momentum, prevent overwhelm, and foster a sense of accomplishment along the way. For example, if your dream is to write a novel, start by setting a daily writing goal, even if it's just for 30 minutes. Gradually increase your output as your confidence and skills improve.

Visualize your success. Before embarking on a calculated risk, take the time to mentally rehearse the situation. Imagine yourself confidently tackling the challenge, overcoming obstacles, and achieving your desired outcome. This mental preparation helps to reduce anxiety, enhance your selfefficacy, and increase your chances of success. Creating a detailed mental script of the event, including potential obstacles and your responses, strengthens your mental preparedness.

Seek support and encouragement. Surround yourself with a network of supportive friends, family, mentors, or colleagues who believe in you and your abilities. Share your goals and challenges with them, seeking their advice and encouragement. A strong support system can significantly bolster your confidence and provide invaluable assistance when facing daunting challenges. Consider joining groups related to your field of interest or your specific goals.

Embrace failure as a learning opportunity. Don't let the fear of failure paralyze you. Remember that failure is an inevitable part of the growth process. Instead of viewing setbacks as defeats, embrace them as valuable learning experiences. Analyze what went wrong, identify areas for improvement, and adjust your approach accordingly. Each stumble helps you refine your strategies and strengthens your resilience.

Remember the story of the tortoise and the hare. The tortoise, through steady persistence and calculated steps, won the race. It wasn't about speed or a single, daring leap, but about consistent progress and resilience. Your journey towards your dreams might not be a sprint, but a marathon, requiring careful planning and a series of carefully measured strides.

Let's delve into some real-world examples. Imagine Sarah, a talented artist who dreams of exhibiting her work. Her fear is rejection. Instead of immediately submitting her portfolio to prestigious galleries, she starts small. She participates in local art shows, seeking constructive criticism from fellow artists and gaining confidence in her abilities. She actively engages with her online community, sharing her work and soliciting feedback. With each positive response, her confidence grows, preparing her for submission to more significant venues.

Consider David, an aspiring entrepreneur with a brilliant business idea but a crippling fear of failure. He doesn't invest all his savings at once. Instead, he starts with a small-scale pilot project, testing his concept and refining his approach with minimal risk. He uses this initial feedback to improve his product or service before launching a full-scale business. This calculated approach mitigates his risk and allows him to learn and adapt as he goes.

Think about Maria, who has always wanted to learn to speak Spanish. Instead of enrolling in a demanding immersion program, she starts with online language learning apps, gradually increasing the intensity of her study. She engages in casual conversation with native speakers, making small mistakes and learning from them. This incremental approach makes the learning process less daunting and more sustainable, encouraging consistent progress.

These examples illustrate the power of calculated risks. They are about progress, not perfection. It's about recognizing that significant achievements are rarely accomplished in a single bound but rather through a series of strategically planned steps. Each successful step expands your comfort zone, builds your confidence, and reinforces your belief in your ability to overcome challenges. The journey may be filled with moments of self-doubt and apprehension, but remember, the reward of achieving your dreams far outweighs the discomfort of stepping outside your comfort zone. The path to realizing your potential is paved with calculated risks, and each step you take, however small, brings you closer to the summit of your aspirations. The key is to start small, build momentum, and celebrate every milestone along the way. Embrace the journey, and the summit will be within reach.

Bouncing Back From Setbacks

We've begun our ascent, taking those carefully calculated risks, inching our way out of the comfortable confines of fear. But let's be realistic: the path to achieving ambitious dreams isn't a smooth, unbroken incline. It's a mountain range, complete with valleys, unexpected ravines, and the occasional blizzard. Setbacks are inevitable. They are not signs of failure, but rather, integral parts of the journey. The true measure of our success isn't the absence of stumbles, but our ability to rise after each fall, stronger and wiser than before. This is where resilience comes in – the bedrock upon which lasting achievement is built.

Resilience isn't some innate quality possessed only by the chosen few. It's a skill, a muscle that strengthens with each deliberate exercise. It's the art of bouncing back, of transforming adversity into opportunity, of viewing setbacks not as terminal ends, but as temporary detours on the road to your destination. Think of it like a seasoned sailor navigating a storm. The storm is inevitable, but the skilled sailor anticipates it, prepares for it, and ultimately, weathers it.

Developing resilience requires a multifaceted approach. It's not a single magic bullet but a combination of strategies, carefully chosen and diligently practiced. First, let's confront the elephant in the room: failure. We often associate failure with weakness, with a lack of ability. But this is a dangerous and limiting perspective. Failure, in its truest form, is merely feedback. It's a lesson, an opportunity for growth, a chance to refine our approach, and to reassess our strategy. It's not about avoiding failure, but about learning from it.

One powerful technique is reframing your perspective. Instead of dwelling on what went wrong, focus on what you can learn from the experience. Ask yourself: What did I do well? What could I have done differently? What new insights have I gained? This process allows you to extract valuable knowledge from seemingly negative experiences, transforming setbacks into stepping stones.

Consider the story of Thomas Edison and the incandescent light bulb. He famously declared that he didn't fail thousands of times, but rather learned thousands of ways *not* to build a light bulb. His resilience wasn't simply his persistence in the face of obstacles, but his ability to learn from each "failure," using that knowledge to refine his approach. He transformed what others might perceive as setbacks into critical data points in his quest for success. His persistent curiosity and adaptability ultimately led to one of the most transformative inventions in human history.

This process of learning from failure is crucial, but it's equally important to acknowledge and process the emotional impact of setbacks. Allow yourself to feel the disappointment, the frustration, the anger. Suppressing these emotions only prolongs the healing process. Find healthy ways to process these feelings: talk to a trusted friend or family member, journal your thoughts and feelings, engage in physical activity, or practice mindfulness meditation. These methods help you process the emotions and move forward. Don't bottle them up.

Allow yourself the space to grieve the loss of a goal or dream, but remember to grieve productively; grief should be a stepping stone, not a resting place.

Building resilience also involves fostering a strong support system. Surround yourself with positive, encouraging people who believe in you and your abilities. These individuals can offer invaluable support, perspective, and encouragement during challenging times. They'll be your cheerleaders, your sounding boards, your shoulder to cry on, and your source of strength when you're feeling down. Their belief in you will help to bolster your own self-belief and propel you forward even when the odds seem insurmountable.

Furthermore, cultivate self-compassion. Treat yourself with the same kindness and understanding you would offer a close friend facing a similar challenge. Avoid self-criticism and negative self-talk. Remember that everyone experiences setbacks; it's part of the human experience. Instead of berating yourself for your mistakes, acknowledge them, learn from them, and move on. Embrace imperfection. Perfection is an illusion, a goal that only leads to disappointment and paralysis. Striving for excellence is commendable, but clinging to the unattainable standard of perfection is self-sabotaging. Accept that mistakes are part of the process and embrace the journey of learning and growth.

Another key component of resilience is maintaining a healthy lifestyle. This isn't just about physical health, although regular exercise, a balanced diet, and sufficient sleep are undeniably crucial. It also encompasses mental and emotional well-being. Engage in activities that bring you joy and relaxation: hobbies, spending time in nature, connecting with loved ones. These activities help to reduce stress, improve your mood, and enhance your overall sense of wellbeing. They recharge your batteries, preparing you to tackle future challenges with renewed energy and determination. Think of it as preventative maintenance for your emotional and mental resilience.

Visualization is a powerful tool for building resilience. Imagine yourself successfully overcoming obstacles and achieving your goals. This mental rehearsal strengthens your belief in your abilities and prepares you to handle future setbacks with greater confidence. Visualize not just the success, but the journey itself, including the inevitable challenges and your ability to navigate them successfully. This mental preparation will build your capacity to face adversity with strength and determination.

Finally, remember to celebrate your successes, no matter how small. Acknowledge your accomplishments along the way, and allow yourself to feel a sense of pride and satisfaction in your progress. These moments of celebration reinforce your belief in your abilities and provide the motivation to continue pushing forward, even when faced with adversity. Success breeds success, and celebrating your milestones, no matter how seemingly insignificant they may be, helps to build that crucial momentum. The accumulation of these small victories contributes significantly to your overall sense of accomplishment and strengthens your resolve to persevere.

The path to achieving your dreams is rarely linear. Expect setbacks, embrace them as learning opportunities, and develop the resilience to overcome them. By incorporating these strategies into your life, you'll not only weather the inevitable storms, but you'll emerge stronger, wiser, and more capable than ever before. Remember, the ability to bounce back from setbacks is a skill you can cultivate and hone. It's the cornerstone of a life lived with purpose, passion, and unwavering determination. It's about the journey, not just the destination, and it's the ability to navigate the challenging terrain that truly defines your character and ultimately leads you to triumph. The resilience you build today will be the foundation for your future successes, allowing you to not only dream and dare, but to ultimately, and triumphantly, *do* .

Cultivating SelfBelief

We've laid the groundwork, acknowledging the inevitable bumps in the road, the setbacks that are as much a part of the journey as the triumphs. We've embraced resilience, the unwavering spirit that allows us to rise after every fall. But before we can truly *do* , before we can translate our dreams into tangible realities, we must confront a formidable adversary: self-doubt. It's the insidious whisper that erodes our confidence, the internal critic that undermines our efforts before we even begin. Overcoming self-doubt isn't about eradicating it entirely – that's an unrealistic expectation. It's about learning to manage it, to silence its nagging voice, and to cultivate a powerful, unwavering self-belief.

Think of self-doubt as a shadow. It's always there, lurking in the periphery, but its power is diminished when bathed in the bright light of self-belief. This self-belief isn't arrogant; it's not about thinking you're better than anyone else. It's about acknowledging your strengths, recognizing your potential, and having unwavering faith in your ability to achieve your goals, even when the path is challenging.

So, how do we cultivate this vital self-belief? It's a journey, not a destination, a process that requires consistent effort and a commitment to self-improvement. It starts with understanding the nature of self-doubt itself. Where does it originate? Often, it stems from past experiences, from moments of perceived failure or criticism that have ingrained negative beliefs about our capabilities. Perhaps a harsh word from a teacher, a missed opportunity, or a personal setback has left a lasting impression, casting a long shadow over our present endeavors.

Recognizing these roots is the first step. Once we identify the source of our self-doubt, we can begin to challenge its validity. Ask yourself: Is this criticism truly accurate? Is it based on facts, or on outdated beliefs and assumptions? Often, our internal critic magnifies our flaws while minimizing our strengths, creating a skewed perception of reality. We're masters of focusing on the negative, while ignoring the countless instances where we've succeeded, even in small ways.

One potent weapon against self-doubt is positive self-talk. This isn't about superficial affirmations repeated mindlessly; it's about consciously replacing negative thoughts with realistic, positive ones. Instead of saying, "I'll never be able to do this," try, "This is challenging, but I'm capable of learning and growing. I'll take it one step at a time." Notice the shift? The focus changes from impossibility to possibility, from self-criticism to self-encouragement.

This positive self-talk needs to be specific and realistic. Vague statements like "I'm great" don't hold much weight. Instead, focus on specific accomplishments. "I completed that challenging project on time, and the client was extremely pleased," or "I successfully navigated that difficult conversation, and the outcome was positive." These concrete examples build a foundation of self-belief, providing tangible evidence of your capabilities.

Celebrate your achievements, no matter how small. Acknowledge each milestone, each step forward, no matter how insignificant it may seem. A completed task, a goal reached, a hurdle overcome – all deserve recognition. This consistent acknowledgment reinforces your self-efficacy, the belief in your ability to produce desired outcomes. Keep a journal, a success log, where you document your accomplishments, big and small. This becomes a powerful tool to combat self-doubt, a tangible reminder of your progress and capabilities.

Seeking support from others is equally crucial. Surround yourself with positive, encouraging people who believe in you, even when you struggle to believe in yourself. These individuals can offer perspective, encouragement, and support during challenging times. They can remind you of your strengths, offer valuable advice, and help you maintain perspective when self-doubt threatens to overwhelm you. This could be a mentor, a close friend, a family member, or a therapist – anyone who provides a safe and supportive space for you to share your struggles and celebrate your successes.

Visualisation is another powerful tool. Close your eyes and vividly imagine yourself achieving your goals. Feel the emotions associated with success – the pride, the accomplishment, the joy. This mental rehearsal not only strengthens your self-belief but also helps you prepare mentally for the challenges ahead. It's about programming your subconscious mind for success, strengthening your resolve and building your confidence.

Don't underestimate the power of small wins. Often, we focus on the grand, overarching goal, neglecting the small victories that pave the way to success. Breaking down large tasks into smaller, more manageable steps makes the process less daunting and provides a steady stream of positive reinforcement. Each small accomplishment fuels our selfbelief, contributing to a sense of momentum and progress. Celebrate each step, no matter how small, as it contributes to the overall success.

Finally, remember that self-doubt is a process, not a permanent state. It's a natural human emotion, and everyone experiences it at some point. The key is not to eliminate it completely but to learn to manage it effectively. Develop strategies to counter its negative influence, to replace selfcriticism with self-compassion, and to foster a mindset of unwavering self-belief. Embrace the challenges, learn from your mistakes, and celebrate your successes. With consistent effort and a commitment to self-improvement, you can transform self-doubt into a source of strength, fueling your journey toward achieving your dreams.

Imagine a tightrope walker. Before they even step onto the wire, a wave of self-doubt might wash over them. The height, the precariousness of the situation – it's natural to feel a surge of fear. But the successful tightrope walker doesn't let that fear paralyze them. They focus on their training, their technique, their breath. They visualize the successful crossing, feeling the balance, the rhythm of their steps. They draw on their past successes, reminding themselves of the times they've overcome similar challenges. They have a support team, a safety net, a source of encouragement. And ultimately, they step onto the wire, one deliberate step at a time, knowing that even if they falter, they have the resilience to regain their balance and continue moving forward. This is the essence of cultivating self-belief – the unwavering confidence to step onto the wire, knowing that you have the strength and the skills to cross to the other side.

Remember, your journey is unique. There's no one-size-fitsall solution to overcoming self-doubt. Experiment with different techniques, find what works best for you, and be patient with yourself. It's a journey of continuous growth and self-discovery, a process of learning and adapting, of celebrating small wins and overcoming setbacks. The path to self-belief is paved with persistence, self-compassion, and a unwavering belief in your own potential. Embrace the challenge, and watch your self-confidence soar. You have within you the power to achieve far more than you ever thought possible. Believe in that power, nurture it, and let it propel you towards the realization of your dreams. The journey may be long, but the rewards are immeasurable.

The Importance of Positive Thinking

We've wrestled with self-doubt, acknowledged its presence, and begun to understand its insidious power. Now, we turn our attention to the most potent weapon in our arsenal against this internal foe: our mindset. Our thoughts, our beliefs, the very way we perceive ourselves and the world around us, profoundly shape our reality. A negative mindset, filled with self-criticism and limiting beliefs, acts as a formidable barrier, preventing us from even attempting to reach our full potential. Conversely, a positive and growthoriented mindset becomes a powerful catalyst, fueling our courage, resilience, and ultimately, our success.

Imagine two climbers attempting to ascend a treacherous mountain. One climber, burdened by negative self-talk, focuses on the sheer cliffs, the potential for falls, the biting wind and the physical exhaustion. Every gust of wind feels like a personal attack, every stumble confirms their inherent inadequacy. They are paralyzed by fear, their progress hampered by their own internal dialogue. The other climber, armed with a positive mindset, also acknowledges the challenges, but instead of dwelling on them, they focus on the beauty of the landscape, the exhilaration of the climb, and the sense of accomplishment that awaits them at the summit. They view each obstacle as an opportunity to learn and grow, each setback as a temporary hurdle. They are fueled by their determination, their positive self-talk bolstering their courage with every step. Who do you think is more likely to reach the summit? The answer is clear. Our mindset is not merely a side note;

it's the very engine that drives our actions and shapes our destiny.

Cultivating a positive mindset isn't about ignoring negativity or pretending that challenges don't exist. It's about consciously choosing to focus on solutions rather than problems, on opportunities rather than limitations, on progress rather than setbacks. It's about retraining our brains to see the world through a lens of possibility, optimism, and self-belief.

One powerful technique is to practice daily affirmations. These are positive statements, repeated regularly, that gradually reprogram your subconscious mind. Instead of dwelling on your weaknesses, affirm your strengths. Instead of focusing on what you lack, focus on what you have. For instance, instead of saying "I'm so clumsy," try "I am becoming more coordinated and graceful with each passing day." Instead of saying "I'm not good enough," try "I am capable and worthy of success." These affirmations aren't just empty words; they are powerful tools that, when repeated consistently, can reshape your self-perception and boost your confidence. The key is consistency – repeat your affirmations daily, preferably in the morning and evening, when your mind is most receptive. Feel the words, believe in them, and allow them to seep into your subconscious.

Another vital aspect of cultivating a positive mindset is gratitude. Taking time each day to reflect on what you are grateful for, no matter how small, shifts your focus from what's lacking to what you already possess. It's a powerful antidote to negativity, fostering a sense of appreciation and contentment. Keep a gratitude journal, jotting down three things you are grateful for each day. It could be something as simple as a warm cup of coffee, a sunny day, or a kind word from a friend. The act of consciously acknowledging these positive aspects of your life will not only uplift your spirits but also enhance your overall well-being.

Visualisation is another potent tool for cultivating a positive mindset. Spend a few minutes each day visualizing yourself achieving your goals. Imagine yourself succeeding, feeling the joy, the satisfaction, and the sense of accomplishment. Engage all your senses in this visualization: see yourself achieving the goal, hear the cheers of the crowd, feel the sense of pride and satisfaction. The more vivid and detailed your visualization, the more powerful its effect. This process not only builds your confidence but also programs your subconscious mind to work towards achieving your desired outcome. It plants the seeds of success, setting your mind on the path towards achieving your goals. Regular practice helps make this a powerful tool, reinforcing your commitment and igniting your motivation.

Challenge your negative thoughts. When a negative thought arises, don't simply accept it as truth. Instead, question it. Ask yourself: "Is this thought really accurate? Is there another way to look at this situation? What evidence supports this thought, and what evidence contradicts it?" Often, negative thoughts are based on assumptions, fears, and past experiences, not on objective reality. By questioning these thoughts, you can identify their limitations and replace them with more rational and positive ones.

Surround yourself with positive influences. The people we associate with significantly impact our mindset. Spend time with people who uplift and inspire you, who believe in your potential, and who encourage you to pursue your dreams. Limit your exposure to negativity, whether from individuals or sources of information. Consciously choose your companions, fostering a network that supports and encourages your growth.

Embrace self-compassion. Be kind to yourself, especially when facing setbacks. Remember that everyone makes mistakes, and failure is not the opposite of success; it's a stepping stone on the path to it. Treat yourself with the same understanding and empathy you would offer a dear friend. Acknowledge your efforts, celebrate your progress, and learn from your mistakes without self-criticism. This is crucial because self-criticism can be the most debilitating force on your positive mindset.

Practice mindfulness. Mindfulness involves paying attention to the present moment without judgment. It's about observing your thoughts and emotions without getting carried away by them. Through mindfulness practices like meditation, you can learn to identify and detach from negative thoughts, creating space for positive ones. Regular mindfulness practices not only reduce stress and anxiety, but also cultivate a sense of calm and inner peace, which are essential for a positive mindset. This allows you to be more present and aware, reducing the power negative thoughts have over you.

Remember, cultivating a positive mindset is an ongoing process, not a destination. It requires consistent effort, selfawareness, and a commitment to self-improvement. There will be times when negative thoughts creep in, when selfdoubt threatens to overwhelm you. But by employing these techniques, by consciously choosing to focus on the positive, you can gradually reprogram your mind, building a powerful foundation for achieving your dreams.

This journey of self-improvement is a marathon, not a sprint. There will be days when you falter, when negativity seems to win. Embrace these days as learning experiences, acknowledge them, and then gently guide yourself back to the path of positivity. Through consistent effort, selfcompassion, and unwavering belief in your ability to grow and evolve, you will gradually cultivate a mindset that empowers you to conquer your fears, embrace challenges, and achieve remarkable things. This is the bedrock upon which your dreams will be realized, a testament to the transformative power of a positive, growth-oriented mindset. The path might be winding, but the destination – a life filled with purpose, accomplishment, and unwavering self-belief – is well worth the journey. So, begin now. Embrace the power of positive thinking, and watch your life transform. The power is within you, waiting to be unleashed.

Breaking Down Goals into Manageable Steps

The journey from a shimmering dream to a tangible reality isn't a magical leap; it's a meticulously crafted staircase, each step a deliberate action leading you closer to your summit.
This is where the magic of action planning truly shines. Think of your overarching goal – that mountain peak you've set your sights on – as a complex landscape. You can't simply jump to the top; you need a well-defined path, a roadmap that guides you through every valley and over every ridge. That roadmap is your action plan.

An effective action plan isn't just a list of to-dos; it's a strategic blueprint, a living document that evolves with you as you progress. It needs to be detailed, breaking down your grand vision into smaller, more manageable chunks. These smaller chunks are the individual steps you'll take daily, weekly, or monthly, each one bringing you measurably closer to your ultimate goal. Without this breakdown, your grand vision risks feeling overwhelming, a daunting task that paralyzes rather than motivates.

Let's say your dream is to write and publish a novel. Sounds fantastic, right? But where do you begin? The sheer enormity of the task – research, outlining, writing, editing, querying agents – can feel utterly paralyzing. This is where your action plan comes in. It transforms this seemingly insurmountable task into a series of achievable milestones.

First, you need to define the milestones. What are the smaller steps involved in writing and publishing a novel?

Here's a possible breakdown:

Phase 1: Idea Generation & Research (1 month): This phase involves brainstorming ideas, researching your chosen genre, developing characters, and outlining your plot. Break this down even further: Week 1: Brainstorming and idea refinement. Week 2: Genre research and competitor analysis. Week 3: Character development. Week 4: Plot outlining and world-building.

Phase 2: Writing the First Draft (3 months): Again, break this into manageable chunks. Perhaps a daily word count goal – 500 words a day, for example – or a chapter-per-week goal. Set realistic targets, allowing for rest days and periods of creative block. Account for editing and revision time within this phase.

Phase 3: Revision and Editing (2 months): This will involve multiple rounds of self-editing, potentially beta reader feedback, and professional editing if you choose to invest in that. Schedule time for each revision stage, including incorporating feedback and making necessary changes.

Phase 4: Publishing (2 months): This phase includes formatting your manuscript, researching publishing options (traditional or self-publishing), preparing your query letter (if going the traditional route), and handling the marketing and launch of your novel. Each step here, too, requires specific tasks and timelines.

Notice how we've transformed a seemingly impossible task into a series of achievable milestones, each with its own timeframe. This is the heart of action planning: breaking the gargantuan into the granular. It's about turning overwhelming ambition into a series of manageable steps, fostering a sense of accomplishment and momentum as you tick each task off your list.

Now, let's infuse this with the principles of SMART goals. Remember, SMART stands for Specific, Measurable, Achievable, Relevant, and Time-bound. Your action plan needs to incorporate these principles at every stage.

Instead of simply stating "Write a novel," a SMART goal might be: "Write a 70,000-word fantasy novel by December 31st, completing at least 500 words daily, focusing on the established plot outline and character arcs." See the difference? It's specific, measurable (word count), achievable (with consistent effort), relevant (to your overall dream), and time-bound (a specific deadline).

Your action plan also needs accountability. Who's going to hold you responsible for sticking to your deadlines? Is it a friend, a writing partner, or a professional accountability coach? Consider setting up regular check-ins, either with yourself through journaling or with someone else to keep yourself on track. This external accountability can be a game-changer, particularly when motivation wanes.

Don't underestimate the power of celebrating small wins. Acknowledge and reward yourself for each completed milestone. It's not about indulging in grand celebrations after every tiny step; it's about consciously recognizing and appreciating your progress. This positive reinforcement keeps your motivation high and prevents burnout. A small celebration – a favorite coffee, a relaxing bath, an episode of your favorite show – can serve as a powerful motivator.

Your action plan is a dynamic tool, not a rigid structure. Life throws curveballs; unexpected challenges arise. Be prepared to adapt your plan accordingly. Don't let setbacks derail you; view them as opportunities to adjust your strategy and refine your approach. Regularly review your action plan, assessing your progress and making necessary adjustments. Are you on track? Do you need to adjust your deadlines or priorities? Flexibility is key to maintaining momentum and staying motivated.

Remember, creating an action plan isn't about stifling creativity or spontaneity; it's about harnessing the power of deliberate action to turn your dreams into a stunning reality. It's about bringing structure and intention to your journey, allowing your passion to flourish within a framework designed for success. Embrace the power of the action plan; it's your secret weapon in the pursuit of your dreams. The path may be winding, but with a carefully crafted action plan, you'll confidently navigate every twist and turn, ultimately reaching the breathtaking view from your summit. Now, let's create that plan! Grab a pen and paper, or open your favorite document, and begin shaping your dreams into tangible steps. Your future self will thank you for it. The journey may be long, but every step, every milestone reached, brings you closer to the incredible reality you're building.

Let's consider another example: imagine your dream is to run a marathon. This seemingly daunting task can be broken down into smaller, manageable goals. Your action plan might look something like this:

Phase 1: Beginner Training (3 months):
Month 1: Establish a running routine, starting with shorter distances and gradually increasing the duration and intensity of your runs. Focus on building endurance and avoiding injuries. Goal: Run consistently 3 times a week, increasing distance by 1 km each week.
Month 2: Introduce interval training to improve speed and stamina. Incorporate cross-training activities like swimming or cycling to improve overall fitness. Goal: Complete a 5km run without stopping.
Month 3: Gradually increase the distance of your runs, incorporating longer runs on weekends. Focus on proper running form and pacing. Goal: Complete a 10km run without stopping.

Phase 2: Intermediate Training (3 months): Month 4: Continue increasing the distance of your long runs. Incorporate hill training to build strength and endurance. Goal: Complete a 15km run without stopping. **Month 5:** Fine-tune your running plan, focusing on pacing and nutrition. Start practicing race-day strategies. Goal: Complete a 20km run comfortably.
Month 6: Focus on maintaining your fitness level and practicing your marathon pacing strategy. Goal: Complete a half-marathon.

Phase 3: Marathon Preparation (2 months): Month 7: Gradually increase your long runs to simulate marathon distance. Pay attention to your nutrition and hydration strategies. Goal: Complete a 30km run. **Month 8:** Taper your training to allow your body to rest and recover before the marathon. Focus on your race-day strategy and mental preparation. Goal: Maintain current fitness level.

Phase 4: Race Day (1 day): Execute your race plan, focusing on your pacing strategy and enjoying the experience! Goal: Complete the marathon!

Each phase consists of smaller, more manageable goals that build upon each other, creating a structured path towards your ultimate goal. Regularly reviewing and adjusting this plan based on your progress and any challenges you encounter is crucial. Remember, flexibility and adaptability are essential components of successful action planning. Furthermore, incorporating SMART goals into each stage ensures that your efforts are focused and measurable, providing a clear path to success. The feeling of accomplishment after completing each step will fuel your motivation to keep going. And remember, the journey is just as important as the destination. Enjoy the process!

Finally, let's consider a creative goal: learning to play the guitar. This can be broken down into manageable steps:

Phase 1: Getting Started (1 month):
Week 1: Purchase a guitar and basic accessories (picks, tuner, strap). Watch online tutorials to learn basic chords (G, C, D).
Week 2: Practice basic chords daily for at least 30 minutes. Focus on proper finger placement and strumming techniques.

Week 3: Learn simple strumming patterns and try playing along with a simple song.
Week 4: Learn a new chord (Em) and incorporate it into your repertoire.

Phase 2: Building Skills (3 months):
Month 2: Learn more complex chords (Am, F). Practice switching smoothly between chords. Work on finger exercises to improve dexterity.
Month 3: Learn simple guitar riffs and melodies. Try playing along with more challenging songs. Experiment with different strumming patterns.
Month 4: Learn basic music theory concepts (scales, notes).
Start writing simple guitar parts or songs.

Phase 3: Mastering Techniques (Ongoing): Continue practicing regularly, focusing on improving technique, expanding your musical knowledge, and exploring different genres and styles of music. Set regular practice goals and celebrate milestones along the way.

This structured approach ensures you're constantly making progress, building your skills gradually, and remaining motivated. This example highlights how even seemingly complex tasks can be broken down into manageable steps, making the overall goal attainable and the journey enjoyable. Remember, every small step you take is a victory, bringing you closer to mastering your chosen instrument and enjoying the music you create. Celebrate your progress, and never stop learning and growing!

Focusing on HighImpact Activities

We've laid the groundwork, mapped out our ambitious landscape, and broken down that daunting mountain into a series of manageable steps. But even with a clear path, wandering aimlessly across the terrain won't get you to the summit. You need strategy, a compass to guide your steps towards the most impactful climbs. This is where the art of prioritizing tasks comes into play. It's not just about doing things; it's about doing the *right* things, the things that propel you forward with the greatest momentum.

Think of your time as a precious resource, a finite commodity you can't replenish. Squandering it on inconsequential tasks is like using high-octane fuel to power a toy car – a tremendous waste of potential. Prioritizing ensures you're investing your time wisely, focusing your energy on activities that yield the highest returns, the actions that bring you closest to your dreams.

One of the most effective strategies for prioritization is the Eisenhower Matrix, also known as the Urgent-Important Matrix. This simple yet powerful tool categorizes tasks based on their urgency and importance. In the top-left quadrant, we have urgent and important tasks – these are the fires you need to extinguish immediately. Think of a looming deadline, a critical client call, or a health emergency. These demand your immediate attention.

The top-right quadrant houses important but not urgent tasks – these are the preventative measures, the proactive steps that prevent future crises. Consider planning, strategizing, building relationships, and investing in your skills. These tasks might not seem pressing in the moment, but neglecting them will inevitably lead to problems down the line. These are the foundations upon which you build lasting success, and they are crucial to long-term well-being. Procrastinating on these will create more urgent and important tasks in the future. Investing time in them will often save you significant time and effort in the long run. It's a preventative maintenance program for your life.

The bottom-left quadrant contains urgent but unimportant tasks. These are often distractions, the shiny objects that grab your attention but ultimately contribute little to your overall goals. Emails, social media notifications, or impromptu meetings often fall into this category. While they might seem pressing, they often rob you of valuable time that could be spent on more impactful activities. Learning to delegate these tasks or simply say "no" is a skill that will greatly benefit your productivity. This is where the discipline to focus your energy comes into play. It is where you cultivate a sense of self-awareness, understanding when to engage and when to disengage from different tasks.

Finally, the bottom-right quadrant represents tasks that are neither urgent nor important – these are time-wasters, pure and simple. Mindless scrolling, excessive TV watching, or unproductive socializing all belong here. While indulging in these occasionally might be beneficial for relaxation and stress relief, they should be kept to a minimum, carefully balanced against your productive activities.

Mastering the Eisenhower Matrix isn't just about ticking boxes; it's about developing a mindful awareness of how you spend your time. It's about making conscious choices, aligning your actions with your values and goals. It's about recognizing the difference between what feels urgent and what truly is. Think about a situation where you might have prioritized a less important urgent task over something truly important. Perhaps it was dealing with an influx of emails instead of finishing a crucial presentation. This highlights the importance of recognizing the deceptive nature of urgency.

Beyond the Eisenhower Matrix, several other techniques can refine your prioritization skills. The Pareto Principle, also known as the 80/20 rule, suggests that 80% of your results come from 20% of your efforts. Identifying that crucial 20% – those high-impact activities – is key. Ask yourself: What are the few vital tasks that, if completed, would significantly advance my progress? Focus your energy on those tasks first. Don't be afraid to say no to other activities, even seemingly important ones. It's a matter of choosing your battles, focusing your energy on the areas that will yield the most significant results. Remember, doing everything well is not the same as doing the most important things exceptionally well. This is the essence of strategic prioritization – directing your efforts towards the most impactful avenues.

Time blocking is another powerful tool. Instead of reacting to demands as they arise, you proactively schedule specific time slots for particular tasks. This fosters discipline and prevents tasks from bleeding into each other. By allocating dedicated blocks of time, you create a structure that supports focused effort, ensuring that you allocate sufficient time to the most critical aspects of your work.

You are essentially creating a framework for your day, transforming reactive behavior into proactive planning. This structure prevents you from getting bogged down in less important tasks and helps you allocate the necessary time and attention to the ones that matter most.

The Pomodoro Technique provides another structured approach. You work in focused bursts, typically 25 minutes, followed by a short break. This technique harnesses the power of focused attention, preventing mental fatigue and maintaining productivity. It's a rhythmic approach to task management that introduces manageable segments of focused work interspersed with short periods of rest. This not only enhances concentration, it combats mental burnout, preventing the decline in efficiency that often occurs when you work continuously for extended periods. This allows you to consistently deliver high-quality work without sacrificing your mental well-being.

But prioritizing isn't just about techniques; it's about mindset. It requires discipline, the ability to say no to distractions and focus on what truly matters. It requires selfawareness, the ability to honestly assess your strengths and weaknesses, and align your actions with your goals. It's about developing a strong sense of purpose, a clear understanding of what you're working towards, and the unwavering commitment to keep moving forward, even when faced with challenges.

Imagine yourself as a sculptor chiseling away at a block of marble. You have a vision of the masterpiece you intend to create. The tools are your time management techniques;

the material is your time and energy. You must be deliberate in your strokes, strategically removing the excess material, focusing on the areas that will bring your vision into sharper relief. You won't achieve a magnificent statue by randomly chipping away at the marble; you must carefully plan each cut, considering its impact on the overall form. In the same way, you must strategically allocate your time and energy, focusing on those high-impact activities that bring you closer to your envisioned masterpiece, your ultimate dream.

Prioritizing tasks isn't about rigid adherence to a system; it's about developing a flexible framework tailored to your needs and goals. Experiment with different techniques, find what resonates with you, and adapt your approach as needed.

Remember, the goal is not to perfectly optimize every minute, but to cultivate a mindful and intentional approach to your work, ensuring that your efforts are aligned with your aspirations. This mindful approach is the key to unlocking your true potential. This intentional use of time creates a ripple effect, impacting not just your productivity, but your overall sense of well-being and accomplishment. By focusing on what truly matters, you cultivate a sense of purpose and control, reducing stress and fostering a sense of achievement. The process of mindful prioritization empowers you to transform your vision into tangible reality.

The Snowball Effect of Success

We've charted our course, prioritized our tasks, and taken the first crucial steps towards our dreams. But climbing a mountain, even with a meticulously planned route, requires more than just a single determined push. It demands consistent effort, a steady rhythm of progress that builds momentum, much like a snowball rolling downhill, gathering size and unstoppable force. This is the essence of building momentum: the snowball effect of success.

Think of that initial, small snowball. It represents your first accomplishment, that initial burst of action you put into motion. Perhaps it was finishing that first chapter of your novel, landing that first client for your business, or simply sticking to your exercise routine for a whole week. It might seem insignificant on its own, a tiny speck against the vast landscape of your dreams. But it is the seed from which everything else grows.

The beauty of consistent action is that each subsequent success adds to the snowball's mass. As you complete one task, the sense of accomplishment fuels your drive for the next. That sense of progress, that tangible evidence of your forward movement, becomes a powerful motivator in itself. It's a positive feedback loop, where each success reinforces your belief in your ability to succeed. You're not just building a project; you're building confidence, resilience, and unshakeable self-belief.

This isn't about pushing yourself relentlessly until burnout; it's about creating a sustainable rhythm, a manageable pace that allows you to build momentum without sacrificing your well-being. Imagine a marathon runner: they don't sprint the entire race. They pace themselves, conserving energy for the final push. Similarly, you need to build in periods of rest and recovery, allowing yourself time to recharge and reflect on your progress.

Celebrating those small wins is absolutely crucial to maintaining this momentum. Don't underestimate the power of acknowledging your achievements, no matter how small they may seem. Each small victory is a testament to your commitment, a reminder of your progress, and a powerful fuel for continued effort. These celebrations don't have to be grand gestures; a simple moment of self-reflection, a quiet acknowledgment of your hard work, or sharing your success with a supportive friend can make a significant difference.

Let's explore some practical ways to nurture this snowball effect:

Track your progress: Keep a journal, use a productivity app, or create a visual chart to track your achievements. Seeing your progress visually is incredibly motivating. It offers a tangible reminder of how far you've come, bolstering your confidence and reinforcing your belief in your ability to reach your goals. The act of recording your progress is, in itself, a small victory, further fueling your momentum.

Break down large tasks: Overwhelming tasks can feel insurmountable, hindering your progress and stifling your motivation. Break down large projects into smaller, manageable steps. This creates a sense of accomplishment more frequently, keeping your momentum strong. Each small win contributes to the larger picture, and the cumulative effect is powerful. You'll find yourself consistently adding to your snowball, steadily gaining speed and confidence.

Embrace the power of routines: Routines provide structure and consistency, which are essential for building momentum. Develop daily or weekly routines that incorporate the actions necessary to achieve your goals. These routines don't need to be rigid or inflexible; they should be adaptable and flexible enough to accommodate the ebb and flow of life. The key is consistency. Small, consistent actions, repeated over time, have a cumulative effect that is incredibly powerful. The snowball gathers weight and speed, effortlessly rolling downhill.

Celebrate every milestone, no matter how small: Acknowledge your achievements, no matter how insignificant they may seem. A small win is still a win, and celebrating it reinforces positive feelings and motivates you to continue your progress. This could be a simple pat on the back, a small treat, or sharing your accomplishment with someone you trust. It's about creating a positive feedback loop that keeps your momentum going.

Visualize your success: Take time each day to visualize yourself achieving your goals. Imagine the feeling of accomplishment, the joy of success, and the positive impact it will have on your life. This mental rehearsal strengthens your commitment, reinforces your belief in yourself, and fuels your drive to keep moving forward.

Your visualization becomes a powerful tool in building the momentum needed to achieve your aspirations.

Don't be afraid to ask for help: Seeking support from friends, family, or mentors can be invaluable in maintaining your momentum. They can provide encouragement, offer advice, and help you stay accountable. Reaching out doesn't diminish your strength; rather, it demonstrates your willingness to learn and grow. This collaboration expands the snowball, adding new layers of strength and resilience.

Consider the example of a writer struggling to complete their first novel. The initial task might seem daunting: hundreds of pages, countless characters, a complex plotline. But breaking it down is key. Instead of focusing on the entire novel, the writer might set a daily goal of writing 500 words. This achievable goal makes the task less intimidating, creating a sense of progress that motivates them to continue. Each day they meet their target, adding another layer to their snowball of success. They celebrate those small wins; maybe a small reward for finishing a chapter, or simply enjoying the feeling of completion after a productive writing session. Over time, their snowball of daily word counts accumulates, and the daunting task of writing a novel becomes a series of manageable accomplishments, leading to the final, triumphant completion.

Or picture an entrepreneur launching a new business. The initial steps—developing a business plan, securing funding, building a website—can feel overwhelming. But by prioritizing tasks and focusing on achievable milestones, they can build momentum. Landing their first client, receiving positive feedback, or securing a small investment, all contribute to their growing snowball. Each success boosts their confidence, fuels their motivation, and propels them toward their ultimate vision. They celebrate every small win, reinforcing their progress and maintaining the momentum needed to overcome the inevitable challenges of entrepreneurship. These small victories strengthen their resilience, making them better prepared for the hurdles that inevitably arise.

The power of building momentum through consistent action and celebrating small wins lies in its transformative effects on mindset. It shifts the focus from the immense challenge of achieving a large goal to the satisfaction of completing small, manageable steps. It transforms the feeling of being overwhelmed by a large task into a sense of empowerment through gradual, incremental progress. This steady, cumulative success reinforces positive self-belief, leading to increased resilience, confidence, and a sustained drive to achieve even greater things. The snowball, once small and seemingly insignificant, becomes an unstoppable force, carrying you toward the summit of your dreams. Remember, the journey is not always smooth, but each small step, each small victory, builds the momentum that propels you towards your ultimate goals. The key is to start rolling that snowball, and soon enough, you'll be amazed at its power. Your dreams, once distant possibilities, will rapidly transform into achievable realities.

Building a Network of Encouragement

The journey towards realizing our dreams is rarely a solitary expedition. While the internal drive and self-belief are undeniably crucial, the power of a supportive network cannot be overstated. Think of a mighty oak tree, its roots spreading deep, drawing strength and sustenance from the earth. Similarly, our aspirations are nourished and fortified by the connections we cultivate. Mentors offer guidance, friends provide encouragement, and family offers unwavering support – each playing a vital role in our growth. A strong support system acts as a buffer against setbacks, offering a shoulder to lean on during challenging times and celebrating our triumphs with equal enthusiasm. This network doesn't merely provide emotional support; it also offers invaluable perspectives, resources, and opportunities that might otherwise remain untapped. The collective wisdom and experiences of those around us enrich our journey, accelerating our progress and expanding our horizons. It's a symbiotic relationship; we gain strength from others, and in turn, we contribute to their growth, creating a positive feedback loop that fosters mutual success.

Building this network is an active process, not a passive expectation. It requires intentionality, the conscious effort to reach out, to build bridges, and to nurture meaningful relationships. This isn't about superficial connections; it's about cultivating genuine bonds based on mutual respect, trust, and shared values. It involves actively seeking out individuals who inspire you, whose experiences resonate, and whose wisdom you can learn from. Consider mentors who have already achieved what you aspire to. Their guidance can save you time, prevent costly mistakes, and accelerate your progress significantly. Mentors aren't just about receiving advice; it's a reciprocal relationship. It's also about offering your own perspective, your unique talents, and your willingness to learn. This exchange creates a dynamic synergy, fostering personal growth for both parties involved.

Think of your friends. These are the people who celebrate your wins, offer a comforting presence during setbacks, and provide unwavering encouragement. They are your cheerleaders, your sounding boards, and your companions on the journey. Nurturing these relationships requires consistent effort – sharing experiences, listening attentively, and offering support in return. It's about creating a safe space where vulnerability is embraced, where you can honestly share your struggles and celebrate your successes without judgment. These friendships don't just provide emotional support; they also offer practical assistance, from brainstorming solutions to offering a helping hand when you're feeling overwhelmed.

And finally, there's the unwavering support of family. Family bonds often represent the deepest and most enduring connections in our lives. While family dynamics can be complex, a supportive family can offer an unparalleled source of strength and stability. They are often the first to witness our dreams, the first to believe in us, and the first to offer a hand when we stumble. Their unconditional love and belief in our potential can be an invaluable asset, providing the emotional bedrock upon which we build our dreams. However, communication is key here. Sharing your aspirations and your journey with your family – honestly and openly – creates a space for mutual understanding and support. Their perspective, even if different from your own, can offer a fresh lens through which to view your challenges. Sometimes, the simplest act of sharing your progress can strengthen these bonds and enhance the support you receive.

Beyond these core relationships, consider expanding your network through professional organizations, workshops, online communities, and volunteer work. These avenues provide opportunities to connect with like-minded individuals, share experiences, and gain access to resources and opportunities that might otherwise be unavailable. Networking isn't about collecting business cards; it's about building genuine connections with individuals who share your passion and can contribute to your journey. Think of it as cultivating a garden; you plant seeds, nurture them with care, and eventually, you harvest the fruits of your labor. The same applies to your support network – you invest time and effort in building relationships, nurturing them with kindness and genuine interest, and eventually, you reap the rewards of a rich and supportive community.

Remember the story of the lone wolf versus the pack? The lone wolf may possess impressive strength and hunting skills, but the pack, with its collaborative efforts and shared resources, often triumphs over greater challenges. The same principle applies to our pursuit of dreams. The support network, much like the pack, offers strength in numbers, shared wisdom, and collective resilience. It's the difference between struggling alone and moving forward collaboratively.

One effective method of seeking support is through active mentorship. Identify individuals who have achieved success in your field or area of interest. Research them, learn about their journey, and then carefully and respectfully reach out. A well-crafted email expressing your admiration for their work and a sincere desire to learn from their experiences can often open doors to a mentoring relationship. Be prepared to show your initiative; demonstrate your commitment to growth and your willingness to actively contribute to the relationship. Mentorship is a two-way street; it's not just about receiving advice; it's about building a relationship based on mutual respect and shared learning.

Beyond formal mentorship, seek out informal support from your network of friends and family. Regularly share your progress, both successes and challenges, with those closest to you. Don't hesitate to ask for advice or simply vent your frustrations. A supportive network should provide a safe space for vulnerability and honest expression. Their empathy, encouragement, and even practical help can be invaluable during difficult times.

Consider also joining relevant communities and groups. Whether it's a professional organization, a volunteer group, or an online forum related to your passion, engaging with like-minded individuals can significantly enhance your support network. These communities offer opportunities for collaboration, knowledge sharing, and mutual encouragement. You can learn from others' experiences, share your own insights, and build relationships that can provide ongoing support throughout your journey.

And don't forget the power of giving back. Once you achieve a certain level of success, consider becoming a mentor yourself. By sharing your knowledge and experience with others, you not only help them on their journey, but you also strengthen your own sense of purpose and fulfillment. This reciprocal aspect of mentorship creates a positive cycle of growth and support, benefiting everyone involved. Giving back reinforces the spirit of collaboration and mutual support that lies at the heart of a strong support network.

Building a robust support network is a continuous process, requiring consistent effort and nurturing. It's not just about finding people who will cheer you on; it's about cultivating genuine connections with individuals who can offer valuable perspectives, practical assistance, and unwavering support. Remember, this isn't a one-time task; it's a lifelong commitment to building and maintaining these precious relationships. The effort you invest in this network will be richly rewarded, fueling your drive, boosting your resilience, and ultimately, propelling you towards the realization of your dreams. Your support network is not just a safety net; it's a powerful launchpad for your success.

Consider the analogy of a ship navigating a vast ocean. A single, solitary ship might brave the storms, but a fleet of ships, sailing together, sharing resources and supporting each other, has a far greater chance of reaching its destination safely and efficiently. Your support network is your fleet, your collective of ships working together to navigate the challenges and celebrate the successes of the journey. Embrace the power of this collective; harness the energy of a unified force propelling you toward your aspirations. Remember, the journey towards achieving your dreams is a marathon, not a sprint. A strong support network is the fuel that sustains you throughout the race, keeping you motivated, resilient, and focused on the finish line. Invest in it, nurture it, and watch as it becomes your most valuable asset on the path to achieving your dreams.

Tracking Your Achievements and Adjusting Your Course

Having established the crucial role of a supportive network in our journey, we now turn to another vital aspect: charting our course and measuring our progress. Think of setting sail on a grand voyage – you wouldn't simply cast off without a map, a compass, and a plan for regular navigation checks. Similarly, achieving your dreams requires a system for tracking your progress, evaluating your results, and making necessary adjustments to your action plan. This isn't about rigid adherence to a predetermined schedule; it's about developing a flexible framework that allows for adaptation and growth as you navigate the unpredictable waters of pursuing your goals.

The first step involves defining clear, measurable, achievable, relevant, and time-bound (SMART) goals. Vague aspirations, such as "becoming successful," offer little guidance. Instead, break down your overarching goal into smaller, more manageable milestones. If your ultimate dream is to write a novel, for instance, your SMART goals could include writing a chapter a week, completing a first draft within six months, and securing an agent within a year. These smaller, achievable goals provide tangible markers of progress, offering regular boosts of motivation and a sense of accomplishment along the way. Each completed milestone acts as a stepping stone, propelling you forward toward your ultimate destination.

Tracking your progress requires more than just setting goals. You need a system for recording your achievements, setbacks, and the lessons learned along the way. This could involve a simple journal, a detailed spreadsheet, or a sophisticated project management tool – whichever method best suits your style and preferences. The key is consistency. Regularly document your progress, noting both your successes and your challenges. This record serves not only as a testament to your efforts but also as a valuable tool for identifying patterns, recognizing obstacles, and refining your strategies. Seeing your progress visually, whether in a journal or a spreadsheet, can be incredibly motivating, serving as a potent reminder of how far you've come and how much closer you are to realizing your dreams.

Consider the power of visualization. Imagine a map with your destination clearly marked. As you achieve each milestone, you mark it on the map, visually tracking your journey. This creates a sense of tangible progress and reinforces your commitment. Similarly, a chart depicting your progress over time can be equally compelling. Visual representations can powerfully impact motivation, transforming abstract goals into concrete realities. Seeing your progress unfold before your eyes can be an incredibly powerful source of encouragement, pushing you onward when facing challenges.

Beyond documenting your successes, your progress tracker also serves as a crucial tool for identifying and addressing obstacles. Setbacks are inevitable on any journey. What matters most is how you respond to them. By carefully documenting your challenges, you gain valuable insights into the patterns hindering your progress. Are you struggling with procrastination? Is a lack of resources preventing you from moving forward? By analyzing these patterns, you can develop targeted strategies to overcome the obstacles and refine your approach. This process isn't about dwelling on failure; it's about using setbacks as opportunities for growth and learning. Each challenge overcome becomes a testament to your resilience and adaptability.

Regular review of your progress is critical. Schedule regular check-in points – weekly, monthly, or quarterly – to assess your achievements against your goals. This isn't just about measuring numbers; it's about reflecting on the overall process. Ask yourself: Are you making consistent progress? Are your strategies working effectively? Are there areas where you need to adjust your approach? Are you adequately supported? These reflective sessions provide an opportunity to recalibrate your course, ensuring you remain on track and adapting as needed. It is during these periods of selfreflection that you'll discover the most profound insights into your strengths and weaknesses, enabling you to optimize your journey.

Adjusting your course is not a sign of failure; it's a testament to your adaptability and commitment to success. Life is rarely linear; unexpected challenges and opportunities inevitably arise. Your action plan should be a dynamic document, not a rigid set of rules. Be prepared to adjust your strategies, timelines, and even your goals as you gather new information and gain new insights. Flexibility is key to navigating the unexpected twists and turns that life inevitably throws our way.

Consider this analogy: Imagine building a house. You wouldn't expect to construct the entire structure flawlessly the first time around. There will be adjustments needed along the way – alterations to the blueprint, the need for additional materials, or unexpected repairs. Similarly, pursuing your dreams requires a willingness to adapt and adjust your course as needed. It's about embracing the imperfections and using them as learning opportunities to refine your approach and build a stronger foundation for success.

Let's delve into specific examples of how you can adapt and adjust. Suppose you've set a goal to write a novel in a year, and after six months, you realize you're significantly behind schedule. Instead of feeling discouraged, take a step back and analyze the situation. Perhaps your initial plan was too ambitious. Adjust your timeline, breaking the remaining work into smaller, more manageable chunks. Or maybe you need to adjust your writing habits. Allocate specific time slots for writing and minimize distractions. Maybe you need to seek feedback from a writing group for constructive criticism and fresh perspectives. The point is, you have several options, and adapting is a key component of achieving your goal.

Consider another scenario: You've set a financial goal, intending to save a certain amount each month. After a few months, you find that unexpected expenses have significantly impacted your savings. Don't give up! Instead, analyze your spending habits, identify areas where you can cut back, and adjust your budget accordingly. Perhaps you can find additional income streams, such as freelancing or a part-time job. The key here is proactive adaptation, not passive resignation.

Remember, your journey towards realizing your dreams is a dynamic process, a continuous dance of action, reflection, and adjustment. It's not a straight line; it's a winding path with unexpected turns and obstacles. Embrace the journey, not just the destination. Celebrate the small victories, learn from the setbacks, and never lose sight of your ultimate goal. By diligently tracking your progress, evaluating your results, and making necessary adjustments, you'll steadily move closer to achieving your aspirations.

And finally, remember that self-compassion is crucial in this process. Be kind to yourself. Recognize that setbacks are inevitable, and that adapting your plan is a sign of strength, not weakness. Celebrate your progress, no matter how small, and allow yourself to feel proud of the effort you are making. This journey is as much about personal growth and selfdiscovery as it is about achieving your specific goals. By embracing both the challenges and the triumphs with open arms, you'll not only achieve your dreams, but also emerge as a stronger, more resilient, and more fulfilled individual. The path to achieving your dreams is a marathon, not a sprint, and remember to celebrate the journey as much as the destination. Your progress tracker should not just be a tool for measuring achievement; it should be a chronicle of your personal growth and transformation.

Recognizing and Addressing Potential Challenges

The path to achieving your dreams isn't a straight, smooth highway; it's more like a rugged mountain trail, filled with twists, turns, and unexpected obstacles. Ignoring these potential roadblocks is like embarking on a journey without a map – you might reach your destination eventually, but the journey will be far more arduous and potentially disastrous. This chapter is about equipping you with the foresight and strategies to anticipate challenges, develop contingency plans, and navigate them with grace and resilience. It's about turning potential pitfalls into stepping stones towards success.

Think of it this way: every challenge you encounter is a hidden opportunity in disguise. It's a chance to test your mettle, to hone your problem-solving skills, and to deepen your understanding of yourself and your capabilities. But first, you must learn to identify these potential roadblocks before they trip you up.

One of the most effective ways to proactively identify potential obstacles is through a process of rigorous selfreflection and realistic assessment. Begin by examining your goals: are they truly attainable within your current timeframe and resource constraints? Are there any hidden assumptions you're making? For example, if your goal is to launch a successful online business, have you realistically considered the competition, the marketing costs, the technical challenges, and the time commitment involved? Ignoring these factors is a recipe for disappointment.

Let's use a fictional example to illustrate this point. Imagine
Sarah, a talented artist who dreams of opening her own gallery. She envisions a bustling space showcasing her work and that of other local artists. However, in her initial excitement, she overlooks several potential obstacles: securing funding, finding a suitable location, navigating the legal and regulatory requirements, and marketing her gallery effectively. Had Sarah taken the time to identify these potential challenges beforehand, she could have developed contingency plans—such as seeking grants, exploring alternative locations, consulting with a lawyer, and crafting a comprehensive marketing strategy—increasing her chances of success significantly.

Another valuable tool is brainstorming. Gather a group of trusted friends, family members, or mentors, and discuss your goals openly. Encourage them to challenge your assumptions and identify potential obstacles you might have missed. Their fresh perspectives can illuminate blind spots and provide valuable insights. The key here is to embrace constructive criticism, not take it personally. Remember, their intention is to help you succeed.

Let's revisit Sarah's situation. During a brainstorming session, her friends point out the highly competitive art market in her city. This leads her to explore alternative strategies, such as creating an online gallery alongside her physical space, thereby expanding her reach and diversifying her income streams. This demonstrates the power of collaborative brainstorming in identifying and mitigating potential obstacles.

Beyond brainstorming, research plays a crucial role in identifying potential roadblocks. Thoroughly investigate your chosen field or industry. Understand the market dynamics, the competition, the regulatory environment, and any potential technological disruptions. This research will not only help you identify potential challenges but also provide you with valuable information to inform your decisions and strategies.

For instance, if Sarah's goal is to sell her artwork online, researching successful online art platforms, understanding their commission structures, and studying their marketing approaches will be crucial. This research will not only reveal potential challenges (like platform fees, competition, and marketing costs), but also provide her with practical insights and strategies to overcome them.

Once you have identified potential obstacles, it's time to develop contingency plans. A contingency plan is essentially a "Plan B" or "Plan C," designed to address unexpected challenges. These plans should be specific, actionable, and realistically attainable. They should outline alternative strategies, resources, and support systems that can be mobilized if your initial plan encounters difficulties.

Returning to Sarah's example, a contingency plan could include securing a part-time job to supplement her income during the initial stages of setting up her gallery, or collaborating with other artists to share costs and marketing efforts. This proactive approach shows that she's prepared for setbacks and is committed to her goals, even when faced with unexpected challenges.

Developing contingency plans isn't about anticipating every possible scenario; it's about being prepared for the most likely challenges. This requires a realistic assessment of your situation, a thorough understanding of your goals, and a willingness to adapt and adjust your course as needed. Remember, flexibility is key to navigating the unpredictable nature of pursuing your dreams.

Imagine a scenario where Sarah's chosen location falls through unexpectedly. Having a contingency plan— perhaps a list of alternative locations she's already researched— allows her to adapt quickly and continue moving forward, minimizing the disruption caused by the unexpected setback.

It's important to note that even with the most meticulous planning, some unforeseen challenges will inevitably arise. This is where your resilience and adaptability come into play. Instead of viewing setbacks as failures, reframe them as opportunities for learning and growth. Analyze what went wrong, identify areas for improvement, and adjust your strategies accordingly. This process of continuous learning and adaptation is crucial for long-term success.

Let's say Sarah's initial marketing strategy doesn't generate the expected results. Instead of becoming discouraged, she uses this as an opportunity to refine her approach. She analyzes her marketing data, adjusts her messaging, and experiments with different channels to reach her target audience. This iterative process of learning from mistakes and adjusting her strategy is key to her eventual success.

Finally, maintaining perspective is crucial. When faced with challenging obstacles, it's easy to lose sight of your longterm goals and become overwhelmed by the immediate difficulties. Regularly remind yourself of your "why"—the driving force behind your dreams—and focus on the bigger picture. Celebrate small victories along the way, and acknowledge your progress, even during challenging times. Remember, the journey to achieving your dreams is as important as the destination itself.

Sarah, amidst the challenges of setting up her gallery, might take time to reflect on the joy she finds in connecting with other artists and sharing her passion. This mindful approach keeps her energized and focused, even when encountering setbacks. It helps her to maintain perspective and continue moving forward.

Identifying potential roadblocks, developing contingency plans, and maintaining a flexible, resilient, and positive mindset are essential ingredients for navigating the challenges you'll encounter on your journey to achieving your dreams. Remember that setbacks are opportunities in disguise. They are chances to learn, grow, and ultimately become a stronger, more capable version of yourself. Embrace the journey, and never give up on your dreams. The rewards are worth the effort.

Developing Creative Solutions

We've established that the path to your dreams is rarely straightforward. It's a winding road, sometimes paved, sometimes a treacherous climb. The previous section focused on anticipating obstacles. Now, let's tackle the core of this chapter: how to *solve* those problems, how to transform those seemingly insurmountable roadblocks into stepping stones to success. This isn't about simply reacting to challenges; it's about proactively developing solutions, thinking outside the box, and embracing the power of creative problem-solving.

The first step is to shift your mindset. Many of us approach problems with a sense of immediate panic, focusing solely on the immediate obstacle rather than the bigger picture. We become trapped in a cycle of negativity, fixated on what's *wrong* instead of exploring what *could be* . Break free from this cycle. Embrace a mindset of curiosity and possibility. See every challenge not as a defeat, but as an opportunity for growth, a chance to learn and evolve. This shift in perspective is the foundation of creative problem-solving.

One of the most powerful tools you can wield is brainstorming. Don't censor yourself. Let your ideas flow freely, no matter how unconventional or seemingly impractical they might seem at first glance. Write them all down, sketch them out, even verbally record them. The goal isn't to find the perfect solution immediately; it's to generate a wide range of potential solutions. The more ideas you generate, the greater your chances of discovering a truly innovative and effective solution.

Think about it like this: imagine you're a sculptor working with clay. You don't start with a perfect statue; you begin with a shapeless lump of clay, and through careful shaping, refining, and removal of excess material, you eventually bring your vision to life. Brainstorming is that initial stage, the shaping of that formless clay. You might start with a hundred ideas, most of which will be discarded, but within that abundance lies the potential for a masterpiece.

Let's illustrate this with a real-world example. Imagine you're an entrepreneur launching a new product. You've poured your heart and soul into it, but initial sales are disappointing. The immediate reaction might be despair, a feeling of failure. But a creative problem-solver would see this as a challenge, an opportunity to refine their approach. They wouldn't just accept the setback; they would brainstorm alternative solutions. Maybe the marketing strategy needs adjusting. Perhaps the price point is too high. Maybe the product itself needs some tweaking. Maybe they need to target a different audience. The possibilities are endless.

The key is to approach the problem from multiple angles. Don't just rely on your own perspective; seek input from others. A fresh perspective can often illuminate solutions you might have overlooked. Talk to potential customers, gather feedback, and analyze the data. Utilize tools such as SWOT analysis to identify strengths, weaknesses, opportunities, and threats. This multi-faceted approach will significantly enhance your chances of finding a workable solution.

Another powerful technique is lateral thinking. This involves approaching the problem from an unexpected angle, challenging conventional wisdom, and considering unconventional solutions. It's about breaking free from ingrained patterns of thinking and exploring unconventional approaches. Lateral thinking often leads to breakthroughs that would have been impossible using traditional, linear problem-solving methods.

Let's consider a different scenario: you're facing a personal challenge, perhaps a strained relationship with a loved one. Traditional problem-solving might involve direct confrontation, a discussion aimed at resolving the conflict through rational argument. However, lateral thinking might suggest a different approach. Perhaps a thoughtful gesture, a heartfelt letter, or a shared activity could mend the rift more effectively than a direct confrontation. Sometimes, a small act of kindness can achieve more than a lengthy, potentially acrimonious discussion.

To further stimulate your creative problem-solving abilities, consider techniques like mind mapping. This visual approach allows you to organize your thoughts and ideas in a non-linear way, connecting different concepts and identifying unexpected relationships. It's a powerful tool for brainstorming, allowing you to see the bigger picture and explore the interconnections between different aspects of the problem.

Imagine you're trying to improve your time management. A mind map might start with "Time Management" at the center, with branches radiating outwards representing different aspects like "Prioritization," "Scheduling,"

"Delegation," and "Elimination of Distractions." Each of these branches can then be further broken down into subbranches, revealing more specific strategies and tactics. This visual representation allows you to see the problem holistically and identify potential solutions you might have overlooked with a more linear approach.

Don't underestimate the power of taking a break. When you're stuck on a problem, stepping away for a while can often lead to a breakthrough. Engage in a relaxing activity, go for a walk, or simply clear your head. Your subconscious mind will continue to work on the problem, often revealing new insights and perspectives when you return to it with a fresh mind. This is often called "incubation," a vital part of the creative process.

Remember, problem-solving isn't a race; it's a journey. There will be times when you feel frustrated, stuck, and even defeated. But it's in these moments that your resilience and perseverance are truly tested. Don't give up. Keep exploring, keep experimenting, and keep believing in your ability to find a solution. Each challenge you overcome will make you stronger, more resourceful, and more confident in your ability to navigate future obstacles with grace and determination.

Let's recap some key strategies: Embrace a positive, curious mindset; brainstorm freely; seek diverse perspectives; employ lateral thinking; utilize mind mapping; and remember the power of taking a break. These techniques, when combined with a resilient spirit and a persistent attitude, will equip you to overcome virtually any challenge you encounter on your path to achieving your dreams. Remember, setbacks are not failures; they are opportunities for learning and growth. They are the stepping stones that pave the way to your ultimate success. Embrace the journey, learn from the setbacks, and never stop believing in yourself. Your dreams are within reach, and with the right tools and the right mindset, you can achieve them. The process of overcoming obstacles is a testament to your strength and resilience, a story you'll tell with pride in the years to come. Each challenge conquered becomes a symbol of your personal growth and unwavering dedication. Embrace the struggle, celebrate the victories, and never lose sight of your ultimate destination. Your journey is unique, your path is your own, and your success is within your grasp.

Adjusting Your Course as Needed

Life, much like a thrilling novel, rarely follows a perfectly plotted storyline. We meticulously plan our chapters, envisioning triumphant scenes and smooth transitions. Yet, the unexpected twists and turns—the plot detours—are often where the true adventure unfolds. Adaptability and flexibility aren't merely desirable traits; they're survival skills in the pursuit of our dreams. They are the secret weapons that transform setbacks into springboards for growth. Rigid adherence to a pre-determined plan, while comforting, can leave us ill-equipped to navigate the unpredictable currents of life. Instead, we must cultivate the ability to adjust our course, to embrace the unplanned detours as opportunities for discovery and innovation. This isn't about abandoning our goals; it's about refining our approach, re-evaluating our strategies, and forging ahead with renewed determination. Think of it as navigating a vast ocean; you may have charted a course, but unforeseen storms and shifting currents will inevitably require adjustments to your sails and compass heading. The willingness to adapt isn't a sign of weakness; it's a testament to strength, resourcefulness, and resilience. It's the difference between being swept away by the tempest and skillfully riding the waves to your destination.

Consider the seasoned sailor, weathered by countless storms. They don't fight the wind; they learn to harness its power. They don't fear the unexpected squall; they anticipate it, prepare for it, and navigate through it with skill and precision. This is the essence of adaptability – not resisting change, but embracing it as an inherent part of the journey. It's about cultivating an agile mindset, a willingness to learn, unlearn, and relearn as the situation demands. The entrepreneur who pivots their business model in response to market shifts, the artist who transforms criticism into inspiration, the athlete who refines their technique after a setback—these are all examples of individuals who have mastered the art of adaptation. They understand that setbacks are not the end; they are simply a call for recalibration, a chance to refine the approach, to seek out a new path to achieve the ultimate aim.

This ability to flex, to adjust and change, is crucial in tackling the inevitable obstacles that stand between us and our dreams. We may meticulously plan our routes to success, but reality often throws unexpected curveballs. A sudden job loss, a change in market trends, an unexpected health challenge – life has a way of throwing wrenches into our well-oiled machines. But it is in these moments, in the face of the unexpected, that our true mettle is tested. It is here that adaptability emerges as the defining factor between success and stagnation. Those who cling rigidly to their original plans, who refuse to acknowledge the shifting landscape, are often left behind. Those who embrace change, who actively seek new solutions and alternative paths, are the ones who persevere and eventually triumph.

Let's look at a few concrete examples: imagine you've spent years building a successful bakery, meticulously crafting your recipes and building a loyal customer base. Then, a new, larger bakery opens across the street, offering similar products at lower prices. Your sales plummet. A rigid approach might involve stubborn refusal to change, clinging to the old ways, and potentially leading to the closure of your business. An adaptable approach, however, would involve assessing the situation, identifying the competitor's strengths and weaknesses, and adjusting your strategy accordingly. Perhaps you could introduce new, unique items, focus on a higher quality, offer personalized services, or strengthen your brand's story to differentiate yourself. You could even consider partnering with local businesses or expanding your services. The key is to not view this as a defeat but as an opportunity to innovate, to become better, and to remain relevant.

Similarly, consider an individual pursuing a career in acting. They might meticulously prepare for auditions, pour their heart and soul into each performance, yet find themselves consistently rejected. A rigid approach might lead to discouragement and abandonment of their dreams. An adaptable approach, however, would involve seeking feedback, refining their skills, expanding their range, networking with industry professionals, and exploring alternative avenues of work within the performing arts industry. Perhaps they could explore voice-over work, teaching acting, or even starting their own theatre company. The key is to remain persistent, resilient, and open to evolving their path towards their goals.

Adaptability is not just about reacting to external pressures; it's also about internal flexibility. Our own beliefs, perspectives, and assumptions can become rigid obstacles hindering our progress. We might hold onto outdated strategies, clinging to ways of doing things that no longer serve us. We might resist new ideas, fearing change or clinging to the familiar, even if it's not beneficial.

To become truly adaptable, we must cultivate a mindset of continuous learning and self-reflection. We must be willing to question our assumptions, challenge our beliefs, and adapt our approaches based on new information and experiences. This involves being receptive to feedback, seeking out diverse perspectives, and constantly evaluating our own effectiveness. It requires a certain level of humility; the ability to recognize that our current strategies may not
always be the best ones, and to be open to alternative possibilities.

The cultivation of flexibility, much like the development of any muscle, requires consistent effort and practice. It's not a passive skill; it's an active one. Here are some practical steps you can take to cultivate this essential trait:

Embrace a Growth Mindset: Believe that your abilities and intelligence are not fixed but can be developed through dedication and hard work. This will make you more open to learning new things and adapting to new challenges.

Seek Out Diverse Perspectives: Actively listen to and engage with people who hold different viewpoints than your own. This will broaden your understanding and help you see situations from multiple angles.

Practice Mindfulness: Develop the ability to observe your thoughts and emotions without judgment. This will help you become more aware of your biases and limiting beliefs, allowing you to challenge them and develop more flexible thinking patterns.

Experiment Regularly: Don't be afraid to try new things, even if you're not sure they will work. Each experiment, even if unsuccessful, is an opportunity to learn and grow.

Develop Problem-Solving Skills: Practice brainstorming, seeking solutions, and experimenting with different approaches. This will improve your ability to navigate unexpected challenges and find creative solutions.

Embrace Failure as a Learning Opportunity: View setbacks not as defeats but as chances to learn and grow. Analyze what went wrong, identify areas for improvement, and adjust your approach accordingly. Don't be afraid to try again, better prepared and more knowledgeable after your missteps. Each failure is a stepping stone on the path to success.

Cultivate Emotional Intelligence: Understand and manage your emotions, as well as empathize with others. This will enhance your ability to navigate complex interpersonal situations and to maintain composure and flexibility under pressure. Emotional intelligence isn't just about understanding your own feelings; it's also about appreciating and understanding the feelings of others.

Develop Resilience: Build up your capacity to bounce back from setbacks. Develop strategies for managing stress, maintaining a positive attitude, and continuing to pursue your goals, even in the face of adversity. Resilience allows you to weather storms, whether internal or external, and come out stronger on the other side.

Adaptability and flexibility are not just abstract concepts; they are practical tools that empower us to navigate the complexities of life's journey. They are the key to unlocking our full potential, to achieving our dreams, and to living a life filled with purpose, meaning, and fulfillment. It's not about avoiding obstacles; it's about developing the skills to overcome them, to learn from them, and to emerge stronger and more resourceful than ever before. Embrace the twists and turns, the unexpected detours, and the challenges that come your way. They are the very essence of the journey, and they are ultimately what shape us into the individuals we are destined to become. Remember, the path to your dreams isn't a straight line; it's a winding road, full of unexpected turns and opportunities for growth. Embrace the journey, adapt to the changes, and enjoy the ride. Your destination is within reach.

Viewing Setbacks as Opportunities for Growth

We've all been there. That sinking feeling in your stomach, the sudden chill that runs down your spine. The moment you realize you've made a mistake. It might be a small oversight, a missed deadline, a poorly chosen word, or a colossal blunder that throws your carefully laid plans into disarray.

Whatever the scale, the initial reaction is often the same: self-criticism, regret, and perhaps even a touch of panic. But what if I told you that these moments, these seemingly devastating setbacks, are actually the most potent catalysts for growth? What if the very mistakes that make us cringe are the hidden keys to unlocking our full potential?

The truth is, mistakes aren't failures; they are invaluable feedback mechanisms. They're not signs of weakness, but rather opportunities for learning and refinement. Imagine a sculptor painstakingly chiseling away at a block of marble. Each chip, each imperfection, informs the next stroke, guiding the artist toward their vision. Similarly, our mistakes illuminate our blind spots, revealing areas where we need to improve our skills, knowledge, or strategies. They force us to confront our limitations, to identify our weaknesses, and to actively seek solutions.

Consider Thomas Edison, the prolific inventor credited with over 1,000 patents. His journey wasn't paved with effortless triumphs. He faced countless setbacks, countless failures in his quest to perfect the incandescent lightbulb. Yet, instead of viewing these failures as defeats, Edison saw them as stepping stones. Each failed experiment yielded crucial insights, eliminating what didn't work and paving the way for a breakthrough. He famously quipped, "I have not failed. I've just found 10,000 ways that won't work." His perspective transformed failure into a process of elimination, a journey of discovery, ultimately leading to one of history's most significant inventions.

The key lies in shifting our perspective. Instead of dwelling on the negative emotions associated with mistakes – shame, guilt, frustration – we must cultivate a mindset of curiosity and inquiry. Ask yourself: What went wrong? What could I have done differently? What lessons can I extract from this experience to prevent similar mistakes in the future? This isn't about self-flagellation; it's about constructive selfreflection, a process of analyzing the situation objectively to glean valuable insights.

Let's delve into some practical strategies for transforming mistakes into opportunities for growth:

Embrace the learning process: Mistakes are inevitable. They're part of the human experience. The more we attempt, the more opportunities we have to stumble. The crucial element is to embrace this process, to see each misstep as a valuable lesson. Don't shy away from challenges; welcome them. They are your teachers.

Analyze the situation objectively: Once you've made a mistake, avoid the immediate urge to beat yourself up. Take a deep breath, step back, and examine the situation objectively. What were the contributing factors? Were there external influences or internal shortcomings? Understanding the root cause will help you develop strategies to avoid repeating the same mistake.

Seek feedback: Don't be afraid to ask for help or feedback from others. A fresh perspective can shed light on aspects you may have overlooked. This could be a mentor, a colleague, a friend, or even a family member. Be open to their insights and use them to refine your approach.

Develop a plan for improvement: Once you've analyzed the situation and sought feedback, develop a clear plan for improvement. What specific steps can you take to prevent the same mistake from happening again? This might involve acquiring new skills, improving your time management, seeking additional training, or simply being more mindful of your actions.

Celebrate your progress: The journey of growth is not linear. There will be ups and downs, successes and failures. It's important to celebrate your progress, no matter how small. Acknowledge the lessons learned and the steps you've taken to improve. This positive reinforcement will boost your confidence and motivate you to continue learning and growing.

Let's look at some real-world examples:

Imagine a young entrepreneur launching a new business. Their initial marketing campaign falls flat, resulting in minimal sales. Instead of giving up, they analyze the campaign, seeking feedback from customers and experts. They discover that their target audience wasn't adequately reached and that the messaging wasn't resonant. Based on this feedback, they refine their strategy, targeting a more specific audience and adjusting their marketing message. The next campaign is a resounding success. The initial failure didn't derail their dreams; it fueled their learning and ultimately led to their triumph.

Consider a musician practicing a difficult piece of music. They make numerous mistakes, struggling with the complex rhythms and melodies. Instead of becoming discouraged, they break down the piece into smaller sections, practicing each section repeatedly until they master it. They seek feedback from their teacher, identifying areas needing improvement. Through persistent practice and focused feedback, they eventually master the piece, demonstrating remarkable growth and skill.

Think about a student failing an exam. They could dwell on their failure, letting it crush their confidence. Instead, they analyze their study habits, identifying weaknesses in their approach. They seek tutoring, improve their time management, and develop a more effective study plan. They subsequently excel in their next exam, demonstrating remarkable resilience and improvement.

The common thread in these examples is the willingness to learn from mistakes, to view setbacks as opportunities for growth, and to persevere despite challenges. This isn't about avoiding mistakes; it's about mastering the art of learning from them. It's about transforming failures into fuel, using them to propel ourselves forward on our path to success. The journey may be fraught with challenges, but remember, it's the process of overcoming these challenges that ultimately shapes us, strengthens us, and ultimately leads us to the fulfillment of our dreams.

It's about cultivating resilience, that inner strength that allows us to bounce back from adversity. It's about developing a growth mindset, a belief that our abilities and intelligence are not fixed but can be developed through dedication and hard work. It's about understanding that failure isn't the opposite of success; it's a stepping stone toward it. It's about embracing the imperfections, the stumbles, the falls – because it's in those moments of vulnerability that we discover our true strength and potential.

Remember the journey is not a straight line. Expect curves, expect detours, expect the unexpected. It's the unexpected that often leads to the most profound discoveries and growth. Each time you stumble, each time you make a mistake, celebrate the opportunity to learn, to grow, to become a stronger, wiser, more resilient version of yourself. Don't be afraid to fall, because it's in the falling that you learn how to fly. The path to your dreams is a journey of continuous learning, and every mistake is a valuable lesson along the way. Embrace the journey, and watch yourself grow stronger and more confident with each and every experience. You've got this.

Keeping Your Eye on the Bigger Picture

We've explored the initial shock of setbacks, the sting of mistakes, and the crucial role of self-compassion in navigating these challenging moments. But even with a compassionate approach, the weight of obstacles can feel overwhelming. It's easy to lose sight of the forest for the trees, to become so entangled in the immediate difficulties that the larger picture fades into a blurry, uncertain background. This is where maintaining perspective becomes paramount. It's the life raft in a stormy sea, the guiding star on a dark night, the unwavering compass that keeps you pointed towards your ultimate destination.

Imagine you're climbing a mountain. The ascent is arduous; the terrain is treacherous. You encounter steep inclines, loose scree, and unexpected storms. At times, you might feel like giving up, exhausted and discouraged by the sheer magnitude of the climb. But if you maintain your focus on the summit, if you keep your eye on the breathtaking panorama awaiting you at the top, you're far more likely to persevere. The momentary challenges – the rocky patches, the fatigue, the unpredictable weather – become smaller, less significant when viewed in relation to the ultimate goal. They're merely stepping stones, obstacles to be overcome, not insurmountable barriers.

This principle applies equally to the pursuit of your dreams. Life, much like mountain climbing, isn't a smooth, predictable journey. There will be setbacks, disappointments, and moments of intense self-doubt. But if you lose sight of your long-term goals, if you become consumed by the immediate difficulties, the path ahead will seem insurmountable. You might find yourself paralyzed by indecision, overwhelmed by negativity, and ultimately, defeated before you even truly begin.

Maintaining perspective isn't about ignoring the difficulties you face. It's about acknowledging them, accepting them, and then consciously choosing to refocus on your ultimate aspirations. It's about remembering why you started this journey in the first place. What is the driving force behind your dreams? What is the underlying passion that fuels your desire to achieve your goals? Connecting back to these fundamental motivations can provide the resilience needed to overcome even the most challenging obstacles.

Consider the example of an aspiring entrepreneur launching a new business. The initial phase is often characterized by long hours, financial uncertainty, and a constant barrage of unexpected challenges. They might encounter technical glitches, marketing setbacks, or even outright rejection from potential investors. If they focus solely on these immediate difficulties, the weight of it all could easily crush their spirit and lead to premature abandonment of their venture. However, if they maintain their perspective, focusing on the long-term vision of their successful business, they're more likely to navigate these challenges with grace and determination. They'll find the strength to adapt, to innovate, and to persevere despite the setbacks. Their vision of a thriving enterprise will fuel their resilience and guide their actions.

Another powerful technique is to regularly visualize your success. Close your eyes and imagine yourself having achieved your goal. Feel the sense of accomplishment, the pride in your achievements, the joy of realizing your dreams. This visualization exercise can significantly enhance your motivation and strengthen your resolve during challenging times. By immersing yourself in the feeling of success, you reinforce the importance of your long-term goals and strengthen your commitment to overcome any obstacles that stand in your way.

Remember, setbacks are inevitable. They're a natural part of the journey. But they don't define you. Your response to them does. When confronted with a challenge, ask yourself: "How does this obstacle serve the larger picture? What can I learn from this experience? How can I use this as an opportunity for growth?" This shift in perspective can transform a setback from a source of discouragement into a powerful catalyst for learning and development.

Maintaining perspective also involves practicing gratitude. When facing adversity, it's easy to focus on what's missing or what's going wrong. However, by shifting your attention to what you're grateful for – your health, your loved ones, your strengths, the small victories along the way – you cultivate a more positive mindset, which, in turn, strengthens your resilience and enhances your ability to overcome challenges.

Furthermore, cultivate a supportive network. Surround yourself with people who believe in you, who offer encouragement and support, and who can help you keep your eye on the bigger picture when you're feeling overwhelmed. Sharing your challenges with trusted friends, family members, or mentors can provide invaluable perspective and emotional support. These individuals can remind you of your strengths, help you reframe your perspective, and offer practical advice to navigate your difficulties. They serve as a vital anchor in the storm.

It's crucial to remember that your journey is unique. Your path to success will likely be filled with unexpected twists and turns. There will be moments of doubt, moments of frustration, and moments when you feel like giving up. But maintaining perspective – keeping your eye firmly fixed on your long-term goals, reminding yourself of your core values and motivations, and nurturing a supportive network – is essential to navigate these challenges with grace and emerge stronger and more resilient than ever before.

Don't get bogged down in the details. The day-to-day struggles, the minor setbacks, the frustrating moments—these are all temporary. They're fleeting storms in the grand scheme of your life's journey. The bigger picture is the sun shining through the clouds, the calm after the storm, the ultimate fulfillment of your dreams. Holding onto that vision, that unwavering belief in your potential, is what will carry you through. Remember the feeling of accomplishment, the pride in your hard work, the joy of finally reaching your destination. Let that vision fuel your perseverance, your determination, and your unwavering commitment to achieving your aspirations.

The road to success is rarely a straight line. It's a winding path, full of unexpected detours, steep climbs, and sudden drops. But with a clear vision and a persistent spirit, you can navigate these challenges and reach your ultimate destination. Remember the lessons learned along the way, the strength gained from overcoming obstacles, and the wisdom acquired from mistakes. Every step, every challenge, every setback is an opportunity to learn and grow.

Imagine a ship sailing across a vast ocean. The journey is long, the waves are unpredictable, and storms are inevitable. But the captain, with a clear vision of the destination and unwavering commitment to the course, navigates the treacherous waters with skill and determination. The ship might encounter strong headwinds, rough seas, and even periods of intense turbulence. But the captain doesn't lose sight of the destination. He or she remains steadfast, adapting to the changing conditions, making course corrections as needed, but never losing sight of the ultimate goal.

Similarly, in your journey towards achieving your dreams, you will inevitably encounter obstacles. These challenges will test your resilience, your patience, and your resolve. But by maintaining perspective, by keeping your eye on the bigger picture, you can navigate these challenges with grace and ultimately reach your destination. Remember, it's not the absence of obstacles that defines success; it's your ability to overcome them with resilience and unwavering determination.

So, embrace the journey. Celebrate the small victories along the way. Learn from your mistakes. And never lose sight of the breathtaking panorama that awaits you at the summit. Your dreams are within reach. Believe in yourself, trust your abilities, and keep moving forward. You are capable of achieving greatness. You have the strength, the resilience, and the unwavering spirit to conquer any challenge that comes your way. The journey may be challenging, but the view from the top will be well worth the climb. Now, go out there and make your dreams a reality.

Prioritizing Physical and Mental Health

The relentless pursuit of dreams, the courageous leaps outside comfort zones, the persistent action—all these are vital ingredients for a fulfilling life. But even the most determined adventurer needs rest stops along the way, moments of replenishment to sustain the journey. This is where self-care, the often-overlooked hero of personal growth, steps into the spotlight. Self-care isn't selfish; it's the essential fuel that keeps your engine running, your spirit soaring, and your vision clear. Think of it as preventative maintenance for your most valuable asset: *you* .

Neglecting your well-being is like driving a car with a warning light flashing—you might get to your destination, but the journey will be bumpy, potentially damaging, and far less enjoyable. When you consistently prioritize self-care, you're not just maintaining your current state; you're proactively investing in your future potential. This investment pays dividends in enhanced productivity, improved resilience, greater creativity, and a profound sense of self-respect.

Self-care encompasses a holistic approach to your physical and mental health. It's not merely about indulging in occasional treats; it's about cultivating consistent habits that nourish your mind, body, and soul. This means attending to both the tangible aspects, like physical exercise and healthy eating, and the more subtle, intangible elements, like managing stress and nurturing your emotional well-being.

Let's start with the foundational pillars of physical health. Regular exercise isn't just about achieving a perfect physique; it's a crucial element of stress reduction and mental clarity. Finding an activity you genuinely enjoy – whether it's a brisk walk in nature, a challenging yoga session, or a spirited game of tennis – is key to maintaining consistency. The endorphin rush following physical activity serves as a natural mood booster, helping to alleviate anxiety and depression.

Beyond exercise, nutrition plays a pivotal role. Fueling your body with nutrient-rich foods is akin to providing highoctane fuel to your car. Processed foods, sugary drinks, and excessive caffeine might offer a temporary boost, but they often leave you feeling depleted and sluggish in the long run. Instead, focus on a balanced diet that includes plenty of fruits, vegetables, lean protein, and whole grains. Think of it as providing your body with the building blocks it needs to thrive.

Sleep, often underestimated, is another cornerstone of selfcare. Consistent, quality sleep allows your body and mind to repair and rejuvenate. When sleep-deprived, your decisionmaking abilities falter, your stress levels escalate, and your overall mood plummets. Aim for seven to nine hours of uninterrupted sleep each night. Create a relaxing bedtime routine that signals to your body it's time to unwind – perhaps a warm bath, some gentle stretching, or reading a book.

Moving beyond the physical, we arrive at the equally crucial aspect of mental well-being. Stress, a ubiquitous part of modern life, can have devastating effects on both your physical and mental health. Learning effective stress management techniques is an indispensable skill. This might involve mindfulness practices like meditation or deep breathing exercises, spending time in nature, engaging in hobbies that bring you joy, or simply setting aside dedicated time for relaxation each day.

Journaling, a simple yet powerful tool, can provide a safe space to process your emotions and thoughts. It can help you identify recurring patterns of stress, track your progress, and gain valuable insights into your own inner world. Writing down your feelings, whether positive or negative, can be cathartic and incredibly helpful in managing emotional burdens.

Cultivating positive relationships is also integral to mental well-being. Surrounding yourself with supportive individuals who lift you up and encourage your growth is essential for navigating life's challenges. Strong social connections provide a buffer against stress and provide a sense of belonging, fostering resilience and happiness.

Self-compassion, the ability to treat yourself with the same kindness and understanding you would offer a close friend, is a powerful antidote to self-criticism. Acknowledge your imperfections, forgive yourself for your mistakes, and celebrate your accomplishments, no matter how small.

Selfcompassion is not about self-indulgence; it's about recognizing that you're human, capable of both triumphs and setbacks.

Mindfulness, the practice of paying attention to the present moment without judgment, can help you to cultivate a greater sense of self-awareness and manage overwhelming emotions. Even a few minutes of daily mindfulness meditation can help you to quiet your mind, reduce stress, and connect with your inner self. It's about appreciating the small moments, the subtle nuances of life that we often overlook in our pursuit of larger goals.

Remember those small wins you've celebrated along the way? Don't underestimate their power. Acknowledging and celebrating your successes, no matter how minor, is crucial for building self-esteem and maintaining motivation. It reinforces positive patterns, reminding you of your capabilities and encouraging you to persist in your endeavors.

Forgiveness, both of others and most importantly, of yourself, is a crucial aspect of self-care. Holding onto resentment and past mistakes only weighs you down, hindering your ability to move forward. Learning to forgive allows you to release the emotional baggage that burdens you, creating space for greater peace and happiness.

Lastly, cultivating gratitude—a practice of appreciating the good things in your life—can dramatically shift your perspective. Taking time each day to reflect on what you're grateful for can enhance your overall mood, reducing stress and increasing your overall sense of well-being. It fosters a positive mindset, emphasizing the abundance in your life rather than focusing solely on what's lacking.

Self-care is a continuous journey, not a destination. It's about incorporating small, sustainable changes into your daily routine that nourish your mind, body, and spirit. It's an act of self-love, a commitment to your overall well-being, and a crucial investment in your potential. By prioritizing selfcare, you not only enhance your capacity to achieve your dreams, but also enrich the quality of your life along the way, making the journey as fulfilling as the destination itself. Remember, taking care of yourself is not selfish; it's essential. It's the foundation upon which you build a life of purpose, passion, and unwavering confidence. So, nurture yourself, replenish your reserves, and continue to dare to dream, dare to do, and dare to thrive.

Staying Present and Focused

We've explored the crucial role of self-care in fueling your journey towards your dreams. We've acknowledged the importance of nurturing your well-being, recognizing that self-compassion isn't a luxury but a necessity for sustainable growth. Now, let's delve deeper into a powerful tool that enhances self-compassion and strengthens your ability to navigate life's challenges: mindfulness.

Mindfulness, at its core, is the art of being fully present in the current moment, without judgment. It's about observing your thoughts, feelings, and sensations without getting carried away by them. It's a conscious choice to anchor yourself in the now, rather than being swept away by the currents of worry about the future or regret over the past. Think of it as a gentle, yet powerful, anchor in the storm of daily life.

In our fast-paced world, bombarded by constant distractions, cultivating mindfulness can feel like an uphill battle. Our minds are often racing, jumping from one task to the next, overwhelmed by to-do lists and anxieties. This constant mental chatter prevents us from truly experiencing the present moment, robbing us of joy and hindering our ability to focus. But the good news is that mindfulness is a skill, and like any skill, it can be learned and strengthened with practice.

One of the most accessible techniques for practicing mindfulness is through mindful breathing. It's a simple yet profoundly effective way to ground yourself in the present moment. Find a quiet space, sit comfortably, and close your eyes if you wish. Bring your attention to your breath—the sensation of the air entering and leaving your nostrils, the rise and fall of your chest or abdomen. Don't try to change your breath; simply observe it. Notice the natural rhythm, the pauses between breaths, the subtle shifts in temperature or pressure. When your mind wanders—and it inevitably will— gently redirect your attention back to your breath. Don't judge yourself for getting distracted; simply acknowledge it and return to your focus.

Even a few minutes of mindful breathing can make a significant difference. It's like pressing the reset button on your mind, calming the mental chatter and fostering a sense of peace. This practice can be incorporated into your daily routine, whether it's during your morning coffee, your lunch break, or before bed. The key is consistency, even if it's just for a few minutes each day.

Beyond mindful breathing, there are numerous other ways to cultivate mindfulness. Mindful walking, for instance, is a wonderful way to engage all your senses. As you walk, pay attention to the sensation of your feet on the ground, the rhythm of your steps, the sights, sounds, and smells around you. Notice the details—the texture of the pavement, the chirping of birds, the warmth of the sun on your skin. Again, the key is to observe without judgment, simply noticing what is.

Mindful eating is another valuable practice. Instead of rushing through your meal, take your time to savor each bite. Pay attention to the texture, the taste, the smell, the temperature of the food. Notice the satisfaction of nourishing your body. This simple act of presence can transform a mundane task into a mindful experience, enhancing your appreciation for the simple pleasures in life.

Engaging in activities like yoga, meditation, or Tai Chi can also greatly enhance your mindfulness practice. These activities encourage a deep connection between your mind and body, promoting relaxation and increasing your awareness of your physical sensations and emotional state. They provide structured opportunities to focus your attention on the present moment, fostering a sense of calm and clarity.

The benefits of mindfulness extend far beyond mere relaxation. Regular mindfulness practice has been shown to reduce stress, improve focus, enhance emotional regulation, and boost overall well-being. When you're present in the moment, you're less likely to be consumed by anxieties about the future or regrets about the past. You become more resilient to stress, better able to manage challenges, and more attuned to your own needs. This, in turn, fosters selfcompassion, allowing you to treat yourself with kindness and understanding, even when you make mistakes or face setbacks.

Mindfulness is not about emptying your mind or achieving a state of complete stillness. It's about acknowledging the constant flow of thoughts and feelings without getting swept away by them. It's about accepting what is, rather than resisting it. It's about cultivating an attitude of nonjudgmental awareness, observing your thoughts and emotions as they arise and pass, like clouds drifting across the sky.

Think about your typical day. How often are you truly present? How often do you find yourself lost in thought, worrying about the future or dwelling on the past? Mindfulness helps you break free from this cycle of mental distraction, bringing you back to the richness and beauty of the present moment.

Imagine the impact this can have on your pursuit of your dreams. When you're fully present, you're more focused, more creative, and more resilient. You're better able to identify opportunities, overcome obstacles, and maintain your momentum. You're less likely to be derailed by setbacks, and more likely to approach challenges with a calm and resourceful mindset.

Incorporate mindfulness into your daily routine. Start small, perhaps with just a few minutes of mindful breathing each day. Gradually increase the duration and incorporate other mindful practices into your life. Be patient and kind to yourself; it takes time and consistent effort to develop this valuable skill. Don't expect perfection; simply strive for progress.

Remember, the journey towards self-compassion and the achievement of your dreams is a marathon, not a sprint. Mindfulness serves as a powerful tool to sustain your energy, enhance your focus, and navigate the inevitable challenges along the way. It's an investment in your overall well-being, enabling you to not only achieve your goals but also experience the joy and fulfillment that comes with living a life of purpose and presence. By cultivating mindfulness, you're not only building a stronger foundation for success, but you're also enriching the quality of your life, moment by moment.

Let's consider some practical examples of how mindfulness can be integrated into different areas of your life. Imagine you're working on a challenging project at work. Instead of letting stress and anxiety overwhelm you, take a few moments to practice mindful breathing. Focus on your breath, observing the sensation of the air entering and leaving your body. This will help to calm your nervous system and clear your mind, allowing you to approach the task with renewed focus and clarity. You might notice that you're able to identify solutions more readily when your mind isn't cluttered with worries.

Or perhaps you're feeling overwhelmed by a difficult personal relationship. Instead of reacting impulsively, take a step back and practice mindful listening. Truly listen to the other person, paying attention to their words and emotions without interrupting or formulating your response. This act of presence can deepen your understanding and empathy, leading to more constructive communication and resolution. Mindfulness allows you to respond rather than react, offering a space for thoughtful consideration and compassionate engagement.

Let's say you're experiencing a period of self-doubt or frustration. Mindfulness provides a space to acknowledge these feelings without judgment. Observe them as they arise, recognizing them as transient experiences, not permanent truths. This self-awareness allows you to approach your challenges with greater self-compassion, understanding that everyone experiences moments of doubt and frustration.

Consider a time when you might have reacted negatively to a situation. Perhaps you snapped at a loved one or reacted impulsively to a challenging circumstance. Now, reflect on how a mindful approach might have altered the outcome. By pausing to breathe, to observe your emotions, and to choose your response thoughtfully, you could have responded with more kindness, understanding, and composure. Mindfulness empowers you to cultivate emotional intelligence, leading to improved relationships and a greater sense of self-awareness.

The integration of mindfulness into daily life is a gradual process. It's not about achieving a perfect state of stillness, but about cultivating a greater awareness of the present moment, allowing you to navigate life's challenges with more grace and resilience. It's about creating space between stimulus and response, allowing you to make conscious choices rather than reacting instinctively. And remember, this is a journey, not a destination. Be patient with yourself, and celebrate the small victories along the way.

The power of mindfulness lies in its simplicity and accessibility. It's a practice that can be integrated into any aspect of your life, enriching your experiences and fostering a deeper connection with yourself and the world around you. By cultivating mindfulness, you're not only enhancing your ability to achieve your dreams, but you're also enriching the quality of your life, day by day, moment by moment. Remember, the journey of self-compassion is a continuous process of growth and self-discovery, and mindfulness is a crucial companion on that journey. Embrace the practice, be kind to yourself, and continue to dare to dream, dare to do, and dare to thrive.

Acknowledging and Appreciating Achievements

We've journeyed through the landscape of self-compassion, learning to nurture our inner well-being and embrace the power of mindfulness. But even with the most steadfast selfcompassion, the path to achieving our dreams is rarely a smooth, uninterrupted ascent. It's punctuated by hurdles, detours, and moments of self-doubt. And that's precisely why celebrating our successes, no matter how small, is not just a pleasant indulgence, but a crucial ingredient in our recipe for lasting fulfillment.

Think of it like this: imagine climbing a mountain. The summit, your ultimate dream, is far off in the distance, a seemingly impossible feat. If you focus solely on that distant peak, ignoring the smaller milestones along the way, you risk feeling overwhelmed, discouraged, and ultimately, defeated. But if you pause to acknowledge each step you take, each challenging incline you conquer, each breathtaking vista you encounter, the journey becomes far more manageable and enjoyable. The smaller victories fuel your momentum, offering much-needed encouragement and reaffirming your capability.

This principle applies equally to all aspects of our lives, from professional achievements to personal triumphs. Did you finally finish that daunting project at work? Did you stick to your fitness routine for a week, even when you felt tired? Did you finally muster the courage to have that difficult conversation? These seemingly small accomplishments are stepping stones toward your larger dreams. They are evidence of your resilience, your perseverance, and your unwavering commitment to self-growth. To ignore them is to disregard the powerful affirmation they offer – a testament to your inner strength and capacity for achievement.

Celebrating these wins doesn't require extravagant gestures or public declarations. It's about creating a mindful space to acknowledge your efforts and appreciate the progress you've made. This can involve a simple act of self-reflection – taking a few moments to pause and savor the feeling of accomplishment. It could be as simple as writing down your achievements in a journal, a practice that not only helps you document your journey but also allows you to revisit and appreciate your progress over time. Consider creating a "success journal," a dedicated space to record your accomplishments, both big and small. Include not only the achievement itself but also the emotions you felt upon reaching it, and even the lessons you learned along the way. This simple practice becomes a powerful tool, a tangible reminder of your capabilities and a source of unwavering motivation for future endeavors.

Consider the feeling of accomplishment after finally finishing a challenging chapter of a book you've been working on, the sheer relief and satisfaction at completing a complex project, or the simple joy of mastering a new skill. These feelings aren't just fleeting emotions; they are valuable resources that fuel our motivation and reinforce our belief in ourselves. By consciously acknowledging these small victories, we're cultivating a positive feedback loop that reinforces our efforts and encourages us to continue striving toward our bigger goals.

The power of celebrating achievements extends far beyond personal fulfillment; it also positively impacts our overall well-being. When we acknowledge our successes, we're essentially rewiring our brains to focus on our strengths and capabilities, rather than dwelling on our shortcomings. This shift in perspective can significantly reduce stress and anxiety, two common impediments to achieving our dreams. It's about building a positive self-narrative, one that emphasizes growth, resilience, and triumph over adversity. Instead of focusing on what we haven't yet achieved, we celebrate what we have, fostering a sense of self-efficacy and empowering us to take on new challenges.

Think of it like this: a gardener wouldn't neglect to water and nurture a young plant simply because it hadn't yet blossomed into full flower. Similarly, we shouldn't underestimate the importance of tending to our inner garden, nurturing our self-esteem, and celebrating each step along the way toward our dreams. Those small blooms are just as important, just as meaningful, and contribute significantly to the eventual blossoming of our full potential.

Let's explore some practical strategies for celebrating your successes. One effective technique is the "Three Cheers" method. Whenever you accomplish something, regardless of its size, take a moment to pause and give yourself three cheers. This might seem simplistic, but the act of consciously expressing your appreciation for your accomplishment, even in this small way, can make a surprisingly significant difference in your mindset and motivation. You can even imagine yourself physically giving three cheers, clapping, and maybe even doing a small victory dance if you're up for it! The physical action amplifies the positive emotions.

Another powerful technique involves sharing your achievements with others. This doesn't mean you need to boast or brag; simply sharing your successes with trusted friends, family members, or colleagues can be incredibly uplifting. Their support and acknowledgment can amplify your own sense of accomplishment and provide further reinforcement for your positive self-narrative. The act of sharing also serves as a reminder of your progress, helping you maintain perspective and motivation during challenging times. Remember, even the smallest milestones deserve recognition.

Imagine a friend who's been diligently working on a novel. They've finally completed the first draft, a significant accomplishment considering the countless hours of work, frustration, and self-doubt they endured. Sharing this with close friends who understand their journey and celebrate their dedication can significantly boost their morale and reinforce their belief in their writing abilities. The same principle applies to any accomplishment, however seemingly insignificant.

Similarly, consider the person who's been working on improving their fitness. They finally managed to run a mile without stopping, a small victory that might seem trivial to an experienced runner, but a monumental achievement for someone just beginning their fitness journey. Acknowledging this victory, celebrating the progress made, and sharing it with a supportive friend or family member can significantly boost their motivation and encourage them to continue pushing their boundaries.

Another powerful strategy for celebrating successes involves creating rituals or traditions. This could involve anything from lighting a candle and taking a moment of quiet reflection to going out for a celebratory dinner or engaging in a favorite hobby. The key is to create a meaningful and consistent practice that helps you consciously acknowledge and appreciate your accomplishments. These rituals can become positive anchors, associating your achievements with feelings of joy, satisfaction, and self-worth. They serve as a reminder of your progress and provide a sense of continuity and stability.

For instance, one person might choose to buy themselves a small gift after completing a significant project, a small act of self-care and appreciation that reinforces their sense of accomplishment. Another might choose to dedicate a special evening to relaxing and enjoying their favorite activities, allowing themselves to fully savor the feeling of success. The act of choosing a specific reward helps reinforce the positive association between effort and reward. This helps prevent burnout, as you're not just focused on the grind; you're actively looking forward to the celebrations.

Creating a vision board is another effective way to celebrate accomplishments. This visual representation of your dreams can serve as a powerful reminder of your goals and a catalyst for action. As you achieve milestones, you can add to your vision board, visually documenting your progress and celebrating your successes. This visual reminder of your achievements can significantly boost your motivation and inspire you to continue striving toward your goals. It serves as a dynamic, ongoing celebration of your journey.

Remember, the power of celebrating successes lies not just in the magnitude of the achievement but in the act of consciously acknowledging and appreciating your efforts. It's about cultivating a mindset of gratitude and selfcompassion, recognizing your strengths, and reinforcing your belief in your ability to achieve your dreams. By consistently celebrating both big and small wins, you are not simply marking achievements; you're building a foundation of self-belief and self-efficacy that will empower you to continue dreaming, daring, and doing.

In essence, celebrating successes isn't about vanity or selfcongratulation; it's about recognizing the effort, acknowledging the progress, and fueling the fire of motivation to keep moving forward on your journey. It's a conscious act of self-love and self-respect, a crucial component in nurturing your well-being and achieving lasting fulfillment. It's the sweet taste of victory that keeps you going, pushing you to reach for even greater heights. So, take a moment, reflect on your journey, acknowledge your accomplishments, and celebrate your successes – big or small. You deserve it.

Letting Go of Past Regrets

The journey to self-compassion isn't just about celebrating victories; it's also about understanding and accepting our past. We all carry baggage – moments of regret, decisions we wish we could undo, paths not taken that haunt our thoughts. These regrets, these ghosts of the past, can cast a long shadow, hindering our ability to move forward and embrace the present with open arms. Forgiveness, both of others and, crucially, of ourselves, is the key to unlocking the chains of the past and stepping into the radiant sunshine of selfacceptance.

Think of your regrets as heavy stones tied to your ankles, slowing your progress, weighing you down in the turbulent waters of life. Each regret is a story, a chapter in your personal narrative that you might want to rewrite. But rewriting the past is impossible. What *is* possible, however, is changing the story's ending. You can choose to release those stones, to forgive yourself for the perceived failures and shortcomings that hold you back. This isn't about condoning mistakes; it's about recognizing them as learning experiences, as crucial steps on your path to growth.

Forgiveness begins with understanding. Ask yourself: What was I going through at the time? What were my limitations? What did I learn from that experience? Often, our regrets stem from actions taken (or not taken) under duress, fueled by fear, insecurity, or lack of knowledge. By acknowledging the context, you begin to separate the action from the person you are today. You were a different person then, shaped by different circumstances and beliefs. You can't change that person, but you can change who you are now.

Consider a woman who always dreamed of becoming a novelist but instead chose a stable career in accounting. She might now regret not taking the risk, wondering what could have been. The regret stems not only from the unfulfilled dream but perhaps from the fear of failure, the pressure to secure financial stability, societal expectations, or even a lack of belief in her own talent. Forgiving herself means acknowledging those fears and pressures – recognizing them as valid parts of her past self – without allowing them to define her present and future self.

Forgiving yourself doesn't mean minimizing the impact of your actions on others. If you've hurt someone, sincere remorse is essential. But remember, holding onto guilt and self-recrimination only serves to prolong the suffering. True forgiveness involves accepting responsibility for your actions, acknowledging the pain you may have caused, and striving to make amends wherever possible. Then, release the self-inflicted punishment. You've learned from the experience; the past is not an insurmountable wall but a stepping-stone to your future self.

Another layer to self-forgiveness involves shifting your perspective on what constitutes "failure." Often, what we perceive as failure is simply a setback, a detour on the path to our ultimate goals. Thomas Edison famously said, "I have not failed. I've just found 10,000 ways that won't work." He didn't view his countless unsuccessful experiments as failures; he saw them as invaluable learning experiences that brought him closer to his ultimate goal.

Embrace imperfection. Striving for perfection is a recipe for disappointment and self-criticism. Accept that you will make mistakes, that you will stumble and fall. It's part of the human experience. Instead of beating yourself up for not being perfect, celebrate your resilience, your ability to rise after falling, to learn from your mistakes and keep moving forward.

Imagine a tightrope walker. They don't expect to walk perfectly without ever swaying or stumbling. They understand that balance is a constant adjustment, a dance between progress and potential falls. They are prepared for the inevitable stumbles and have the skill and confidence to recover their balance. Similarly, our journey towards our dreams is a tightrope walk. Embrace the wobbles, the stumbles, the near misses. They are all part of the process of learning and growing. Learning to self-forgive is mastering the art of maintaining balance in the midst of life's inevitable stumbles.

Self-acceptance is inextricably linked to self-forgiveness. It's about acknowledging your strengths and weaknesses, your flaws and imperfections, without judgment or self-criticism. It's about seeing yourself as a whole person, not just the sum of your accomplishments or failures. Self-acceptance means embracing all aspects of yourself, the good, the bad, and the ugly. It's recognizing that you are worthy of love and compassion regardless of your imperfections.

This journey of self-acceptance might involve journaling. Writing down your regrets, exploring the emotions associated with them, and identifying the lessons learned can be incredibly cathartic. You might also find it helpful to talk to a therapist or counselor who can provide guidance and support as you navigate these complex emotions. Sometimes, simply articulating your feelings to a trusted friend or family member can be a significant step towards self-forgiveness.

Remember, self-compassion isn't a destination but a continuous practice. It's about being kind to yourself, particularly during difficult times. It's about treating yourself with the same empathy and understanding you would offer a close friend facing similar challenges. It's about giving yourself permission to feel your emotions, to acknowledge your struggles without judgment, and to recognize your inherent worthiness, regardless of your past mistakes or perceived failures.

Cultivating self-compassion involves self-care. This isn't about indulging in luxuries; it's about prioritizing activities that nurture your physical, mental, and emotional well-being. This might include regular exercise, mindful meditation, healthy eating habits, spending time in nature, engaging in hobbies you enjoy, or pursuing creative outlets. These practices are not just self-indulgent; they are crucial tools for building resilience, coping with stress, and nurturing your inner strength.

Develop a ritual of self-reflection. Each evening, take a few minutes to reflect on your day. Acknowledge your accomplishments, big and small. Identify any areas where you could have been kinder to yourself. This regular practice can help you cultivate a more compassionate and forgiving inner voice. The more you practice self-compassion, the easier it will become, the more it will become a natural part of your way of being. It will flow into your relationships with others, enriching your connections and deepening your capacity for empathy and understanding.

Imagine a garden. A garden requires constant nurturing, weeding out the unwanted, and tending to the flowers and plants. Self-compassion is like tending to your own inner garden. You need to cultivate the good, weed out the selfcriticism and regret, and nurture your own growth. The flowers of self-acceptance and forgiveness will only bloom if you consistently nurture the soil of your being.

The journey of self-forgiveness and self-acceptance is a marathon, not a sprint. There will be days when you stumble, days when the weight of the past feels overwhelming. Be patient with yourself. Celebrate the small victories, acknowledge the progress you've made, and remember that you are worthy of love and compassion, even – especially – when you make mistakes. Embrace your imperfections, forgive your past self, and move forward with unwavering self-compassion. The path to your dreams awaits.

Focusing on the Good in Your Life

Having embraced self-forgiveness and navigated the complexities of self-acceptance, we now stand at the threshold of a new and profoundly empowering concept: cultivating gratitude and positivity. This isn't about burying our heads in the sand and ignoring life's challenges; rather, it's about shifting our perspective, choosing to focus on the good amidst the inevitable storms. It's about actively seeking out and appreciating the blessings that surround us, both big and small, transforming our inner landscape from one of scarcity and negativity to one of abundance and joy.

Think of your mind as a garden. If you only tend to the weeds – the anxieties, the regrets, the negative self-talk – they will quickly overrun the entire space, choking out any potential for growth and beauty. But if you dedicate time and energy to cultivating the flowers – the moments of joy, the expressions of gratitude, the positive affirmations – your garden will blossom, transforming your inner world into a vibrant and flourishing landscape.

This cultivation begins with a simple yet powerful practice: keeping a gratitude journal. Each day, take a few moments to reflect on the things you're grateful for. These don't have to be monumental events; they can be as simple as a warm cup of coffee on a chilly morning, a kind word from a friend, the laughter of a loved one, the beauty of a sunset, or even the simple comfort of a soft bed. The key is to consciously acknowledge these positive aspects of your day, anchoring yourself in the present moment and appreciating the abundance that already surrounds you.

Don't underestimate the power of small acts of gratitude. A quick thank-you note to a colleague, a heartfelt compliment to a stranger, or a simple expression of appreciation to a family member can create ripples of positivity, not only for the recipient but also for yourself. By expressing gratitude, we activate a feedback loop of positive emotions, reinforcing the feeling of well-being and contentment. This act of acknowledging the good fosters a sense of interconnectedness, reminding us that we are not alone in our journey and that there is much to be thankful for.

Beyond the journal, expand your practice into mindful moments. Take time each day, even just for five minutes, to engage in a mindful activity that allows you to fully appreciate the present. This could involve savoring a cup of tea, listening to your favorite music, or taking a walk in nature, paying close attention to the sights, sounds, and sensations around you. By slowing down and truly immersing yourself in the experience, you create space for gratitude to flourish. The simple act of noticing – noticing the warmth of the sun on your skin, the scent of flowers in the air, the gentle breeze rustling through the leaves – can profoundly shift your perspective and foster a deeper appreciation for the beauty in your life.

Cultivating positivity isn't about ignoring the negative aspects of life, but rather about consciously choosing to focus on the positive. This doesn't mean suppressing your feelings or pretending that everything is perfect. It's about acknowledging the challenges you face while simultaneously focusing on the solutions, the opportunities, and the strength within you to overcome obstacles. When negative thoughts arise, challenge them. Ask yourself: Is this thought helpful? Is it based on fact or assumption? If it's unhelpful and based on assumption, gently redirect your attention to a more positive and constructive thought.

This intentional shift in focus requires practice. Our minds are naturally wired to gravitate towards negativity – it's a survival mechanism designed to keep us safe from potential threats. But we can rewire our brains through conscious effort and consistent practice. Start small, focusing on one or two positive aspects of your day, and gradually expand your practice as you become more comfortable. Celebrate small victories, acknowledging your progress and appreciating the positive changes you're experiencing.

Remember that positivity is not about forced happiness or unrealistic expectations of perfection. It's about cultivating a resilient mindset that allows you to navigate life's challenges with grace, strength, and a sense of hope. It's about embracing the full spectrum of human emotion, acknowledging the negative feelings without letting them define your experience.

Imagine your life as a tapestry woven with threads of different colors – some bright and vibrant, others dark and somber. The negative experiences are an integral part of the tapestry, adding depth and complexity to the overall design. However, by focusing on the positive threads – the moments of joy, gratitude, and accomplishment – you create a masterpiece that is both beautiful and meaningful.

To further deepen your practice of gratitude and positivity, consider incorporating affirmations into your daily routine. Affirmations are positive statements that you repeat to yourself, reinforcing beliefs and attitudes that promote wellbeing and self-confidence. Choose affirmations that resonate with you personally and repeat them several times a day, visualizing yourself embodying the qualities you're affirming.

For example, you might use affirmations like: "I am grateful for the good in my life," "I am strong and capable," "I am worthy of love and happiness," "I choose to focus on the positive," or "I am attracting abundance into my life." These affirmations can help reprogram your subconscious mind, creating a more positive and empowering internal dialogue.

Furthermore, surround yourself with positive influences. Spend time with people who uplift and inspire you, who celebrate your accomplishments and support your growth. Limit your exposure to negativity, whether it's through social media, news, or relationships that drain your energy. Cultivate relationships that nourish your soul and nurture your spirit.

Remember, cultivating gratitude and positivity is a journey, not a destination. There will be days when it feels challenging to maintain a positive perspective. There will be times when you feel overwhelmed by negative emotions. On these days, be kind to yourself. Acknowledge your feelings without judgment and gently redirect your focus back to the positive aspects of your life.

Practice self-compassion, remembering that it's okay to have bad days. It's okay to feel overwhelmed or discouraged at times. What matters is your willingness to consistently choose gratitude and positivity, even amidst the challenges. This persistent effort is what will transform your mindset, allowing you to live a life filled with joy, contentment, and a deep sense of appreciation for the incredible journey you are on.

Embrace the power of small acts of kindness. Performing random acts of kindness not only benefits the recipient but also enhances your own sense of well-being. Helping others, whether it's through volunteering, donating to charity, or simply offering a helping hand to someone in need, creates a powerful ripple effect of positivity. It shifts your focus outward, reminding you of the interconnectedness of life and the abundance of opportunities to make a positive impact.

Finally, remember that the journey towards self-compassion, gratitude, and positivity is deeply personal. There's no right or wrong way to do it; the most important aspect is to find practices that resonate with you and that you can consistently incorporate into your daily life. Experiment with different techniques, find what works best for you, and create a personalized approach that supports your overall well-being. Your journey is unique, and your path to a life of self-love, gratitude, and positivity is yours to create. Embrace the process, celebrate your progress, and never underestimate the transformative

power of choosing to focus on the good. The path to your dreams is paved with gratitude and positive intention; embrace the journey and watch your dreams bloom.
Maintaining LongTerm Motivation

The thrill of setting a goal, the exhilarating rush of taking the first steps – these are the moments that fuel our initial drive. But the path to achieving a lifelong dream is rarely a straight line. It's a winding road, full of unexpected twists and turns, uphill climbs, and valleys of self-doubt. Sustaining the momentum, keeping the flame of motivation burning brightly throughout this journey, is the true test of our commitment and resilience. It's not about the initial burst of energy; it's about the consistent, unwavering dedication that carries you through the inevitable challenges.

Think of it like this: imagine you're embarking on a challenging hike to reach a breathtaking summit. The initial ascent might be invigorating, fueled by the anticipation of the stunning view awaiting you. But as you climb higher, the path becomes steeper, the air thinner, and fatigue sets in. The spectacular view becomes a distant promise, and the temptation to turn back, to settle for the comfort of the valley below, becomes almost overpowering. This is where maintaining momentum becomes crucial. It's the grit that keeps your boots moving, one step at a time, even when the summit seems miles away.

So how do we cultivate this unwavering dedication, this inner strength that propels us forward even when the going gets tough? It's not a matter of sheer willpower alone; it's a multifaceted approach that requires a strategic blend of internal and external factors.

First, we must recognize that motivation isn't a constant; it's a fluctuating force, ebbs and flows like the tide. There will be days when the energy surges, propelling you forward with unstoppable force, and other days when the flame flickers, threatening to extinguish altogether. Accepting this ebb and flow is the first step. Don't beat yourself up for those days when motivation wanes; acknowledge them, understand their causes, and then gently nudge yourself back onto the path.

One powerful tool for sustaining motivation is the power of **small, consistent wins.** Instead of focusing solely on the monumental end goal, break it down into smaller, manageable milestones. Each small victory, no matter how insignificant it may seem, serves as a powerful affirmation, a boost of confidence that keeps you moving forward. Imagine painting a large mural – the completed masterpiece may seem overwhelming, but each brushstroke, each completed section, builds towards the final vision. Celebrate these smaller wins, acknowledge your progress, and let that positive reinforcement fuel your continued efforts.

Furthermore, **regular reflection and recalibration** are crucial for maintaining long-term motivation. Schedule dedicated time for self-assessment. Ask yourself: Am I still on track with my goals? What obstacles have I encountered, and how have I overcome them? What adjustments do I need to make to my approach? This reflective process allows you to identify potential roadblocks early on, preventing them from derailing your progress. It also ensures that you're staying true to your core values and that your goals still resonate with your evolving self. Life changes, and your aspirations may shift as you grow and learn.

Building a **strong support system** is another critical element. Surround yourself with positive, encouraging individuals who believe in your dreams and offer unwavering support. This could be a mentor, a close friend, a family member, or a supportive community. These individuals provide invaluable encouragement during times of doubt, offering a listening ear, a fresh perspective, and the motivation you need to keep pushing forward. Sharing your journey with others also creates a sense of accountability, making you more likely to stay committed to your goals.

The power of **visualization** should not be underestimated. Regularly visualize yourself achieving your goals, focusing on the feelings and experiences associated with success. This mental rehearsal strengthens your belief in your ability to achieve your aspirations and reinforces your commitment to the process. Make it a habit to spend a few minutes each day immersing yourself in the feeling of accomplishment, imagining the positive impact your success will have on your life and the lives of those around you.

Flexibility and adaptability are also paramount. Life rarely unfolds exactly as planned. Unexpected challenges and obstacles will inevitably arise, threatening to derail your progress. Develop the ability to adapt, to adjust your course when necessary, without losing sight of your ultimate goal. Treat setbacks not as failures but as valuable learning opportunities. Analyze what went wrong, learn from your mistakes, and adjust your strategy accordingly. Remember, it's not about avoiding challenges; it's about learning to navigate them with grace and resilience.

Moreover, **self-compassion** is vital for sustaining long-term motivation. Be kind to yourself, especially during moments of doubt and self-criticism. Acknowledge that setbacks and imperfections are a natural part of the journey. Don't dwell on your mistakes; learn from them and move forward. Treat yourself with the same understanding and empathy you would offer a close friend facing similar challenges.

Finally, remember that the journey is as important as the destination. Focus not only on the end goal but also on the personal growth and transformation you experience along the way. Savor the small victories, appreciate the lessons learned, and find fulfillment in the process of striving towards your dreams. The journey itself is a testament to your resilience, your determination, and your unwavering commitment to self-improvement. Embrace the challenges, celebrate the successes, and relish the transformative power of pursuing your dreams. It's not just about reaching the summit; it's about the person you become in the process of climbing. The view from the top is incredible, but the journey itself is a lifelong adventure filled with opportunities for growth, self-discovery, and the unwavering satisfaction of living a life aligned with your true purpose. This enduring commitment, this consistent perseverance, is what truly defines success.

Embracing Lifelong Personal Development

The summit conquered, the dream realized – that's the image we often conjure when envisioning success. But the truth is, reaching the peak is just the beginning of a breathtaking vista, a panoramic view of opportunities for continued growth and fulfillment. True success isn't a destination; it's a journey, a continuous evolution that demands a commitment to lifelong learning and personal development. Think of your life's aspirations not as isolated peaks to conquer, but as a majestic mountain range, each summit offering a new and challenging ascent, a new perspective, and a deeper understanding of yourself and your capabilities.

This journey of continuous learning isn't about chasing fleeting trends or accumulating meaningless qualifications. It's about cultivating a mindset of curiosity, a thirst for knowledge that fuels your personal and professional evolution. It's about consistently seeking new experiences, challenging your assumptions, and embracing the unknown with a sense of adventure rather than fear. This commitment to lifelong growth isn't a chore; it's the very essence of a life well-lived, a life brimming with purpose and meaning. It's the fuel that keeps the fire of passion burning brightly, even when the path becomes steep and arduous.

Consider the seasoned craftsman, their hands weathered by years of dedication, their expertise honed through countless hours of practice and experimentation. They haven't simply mastered a skill; they've cultivated a deep and abiding love for their craft, constantly seeking new techniques, new materials, new ways to refine their artistry. Their journey is a testament to the power of lifelong learning, a demonstration that mastery is a continuous process, not a final destination.

The same principle applies to every facet of life. Whether you're an artist honing your technique, a scientist exploring uncharted territories, or a business leader navigating complex markets, the pursuit of knowledge and selfimprovement is paramount. In the ever-evolving landscape of the modern world, complacency is the enemy of progress. Staying stagnant, clinging to outdated skills and perspectives, will leave you ill-equipped to navigate the challenges and seize the opportunities that lie ahead.

Think about the professional athlete. Their success isn't solely determined by innate talent; it's fueled by rigorous training, a relentless pursuit of self-improvement, a dedication to constantly refining their skills. They study their opponents, analyze their weaknesses, and embrace new training techniques to stay ahead of the competition. They are constantly learning, constantly adapting, constantly evolving. This isn't just about winning medals; it's about pushing the boundaries of human potential.

Embracing lifelong personal development is not merely about acquiring new knowledge; it's about cultivating a growth mindset, a belief that your abilities and intelligence can be developed through dedication and hard work. It's about embracing challenges, seeing them not as obstacles but as opportunities for growth and learning. It's about viewing setbacks not as failures, but as valuable lessons, stepping stones on the path towards mastery. It's about developing resilience, the ability to bounce back from adversity and emerge stronger and wiser.

This mindset shift is crucial because it transforms the very way you approach life's challenges. Instead of fearing failure, you embrace it as a natural part of the learning process. Instead of shying away from difficult tasks, you see them as opportunities to expand your capabilities and test your limits. This doesn't mean you should recklessly disregard sensible precautions or repeatedly make the same mistakes, but rather that you should learn from your setbacks, adapt your approach, and persevere. The journey towards mastery is rarely a linear one, marked by continuous progress. Expect setbacks, adjust, and learn from each stumble. That resilience, that persistent dedication to improvement, is the hallmark of true success.

How then do we cultivate this mindset of continuous learning and embrace lifelong personal development? It starts with cultivating curiosity, a genuine desire to learn and grow. Ask yourself questions, challenge your assumptions, and seek out new experiences. Read widely, not just within your field of expertise, but across disciplines. Explore different cultures, engage in meaningful conversations, and immerse yourself in environments that expand your horizons. The world is a vast and endlessly fascinating place, brimming with knowledge and perspectives waiting to be discovered.

Formal education is a powerful tool, but it's just one piece of the puzzle. Consider informal learning opportunities: workshops, seminars, online courses, podcasts, and mentorship programs. These avenues offer flexible and accessible ways to acquire new skills and knowledge, allowing you to tailor your learning journey to your specific interests and goals. Embrace the power of online communities, connecting with others who share your passions, exchanging ideas, and collaborating on projects.

Seek out mentors, experienced individuals who can guide and inspire you on your path. Their wisdom and insights can provide invaluable support and direction, accelerating your learning and helping you avoid common pitfalls. Mentorship transcends mere instruction; it's a relationship built on mutual respect, trust, and a shared commitment to growth. Actively seek out individuals whose achievements and perspectives resonate with you.

Furthermore, actively seek feedback from others. Don't be afraid to ask for constructive criticism; it's an invaluable tool for identifying areas for improvement and refining your skills. Honest feedback, even when challenging, can be a catalyst for significant personal and professional growth. Embrace the discomfort of vulnerability and use it as an opportunity to learn and evolve.

Continuous learning isn't just about acquiring knowledge; it's also about applying that knowledge to real-world situations. Seek opportunities to put your new skills and insights into practice, challenging yourself to step outside your comfort zone and tackle projects that push your boundaries. This practical application is what truly solidifies your learning, transforming theoretical knowledge into tangible skills and experiences.

Remember, continuous learning is not a race. It's a marathon. There will be days when your motivation wanes, when the challenges seem insurmountable, when the sheer volume of information seems overwhelming. That's perfectly normal. It's during these moments that the cultivation of self-compassion and persistence are most crucial. Forgive yourself for setbacks, and gently nudge yourself back onto the path. Celebrate small victories, appreciate the progress you've made, and remember the long-term vision that fuels your journey.

The path to achieving your dreams is a lifelong adventure, a continuous journey of learning, growth, and transformation. Embrace the challenges, celebrate the victories, and never stop exploring the vast and endlessly fascinating landscape of human potential. The view from the summit is breathtaking, but the journey itself, the ongoing commitment to personal and professional growth, is what truly defines a life well-lived. It's the ongoing pursuit of excellence, the relentless curiosity, and the unwavering dedication to lifelong learning that makes the climb worthwhile, and the summit all the more rewarding. The true measure of success isn't reaching the top, it's the person you become in the process of the climb itself. And that journey, my friends, is a lifelong endeavor.

Sharing Your Success and Inspiring Others

The exhilarating rush of achieving a lifelong dream is undeniably intoxicating. That moment of triumph, the culmination of years of hard work, dedication, and unwavering belief in yourself – it's a feeling etched into the very fabric of your being. But as the celebratory confetti settles and the applause fades, a profound realization dawns: this isn't just *your* victory. Your journey, your struggles, your triumphs – they hold the power to ignite a spark in others, to inspire them to chase their own improbable dreams. This is where the next chapter of your journey begins: giving back.

Giving back isn't merely an act of altruism; it's a deeply fulfilling extension of your own personal growth. It's about recognizing that the skills, knowledge, and resilience you've cultivated on your path to success aren't meant to be hoarded like precious jewels. They are meant to be shared, to be used as tools to empower others to embark on their own incredible adventures. Imagine the ripple effect: your success inspiring others, their success inspiring more, creating a cascading wave of positive change that touches countless lives.

Consider the young woman who, after years of tireless work, finally launched her successful bakery. The aroma of freshly baked bread filling her charming storefront, a testament to her unwavering dedication. Her journey wasn't easy. She faced skepticism, setbacks, and moments of doubt. Yet, she persevered, fueled by her passion and an unshakeable belief in her abilities. Now, instead of simply basking in the warmth of her success, she uses her platform to mentor aspiring entrepreneurs, offering workshops and sharing her invaluable experience, guiding others through the labyrinthine paths of starting a business. She doesn't just teach them the techniques of baking; she teaches them the resilience needed to overcome obstacles, the importance of perseverance in the face of adversity, and the power of believing in oneself.

Or think about the man who, after overcoming a debilitating illness, dedicated his life to raising awareness and funds for research. His journey was a testament to the human spirit's incredible capacity for resilience and determination. His struggle was not just his own; it became a symbol of hope for others battling similar conditions. His success wasn't measured in financial wealth; it was measured in the lives he touched, the hope he instilled, and the progress he facilitated in the fight against disease. He shares his story openly, not to wallow in past suffering, but to inspire others to confront their own challenges with courage and determination, reminding them that even in the darkest of times, hope remains a powerful force.

These are not isolated instances; they are testaments to the transformative power of sharing your success. It's about recognizing that your journey holds a unique message, a narrative that can resonate deeply with those who are still on their own paths. It's about extending a helping hand, sharing your wisdom, and illuminating the way for others. The act of giving back is not just about financial contributions; it's about sharing your time, your expertise, your experience, your very essence.

This act of giving back can manifest in countless ways. Perhaps you volunteer at a local charity, sharing your skills and expertise to support a cause you believe in. Or maybe you mentor young people, guiding them towards their goals and helping them overcome obstacles. You might choose to share your knowledge through workshops, online courses, or simply by offering advice and support to those who need it. Your actions might range from writing a blog post sharing your struggles and triumphs, offering inspiration to those navigating similar challenges, to giving motivational speeches at schools and conferences, empowering individuals to take charge of their lives.

The key is to find a way that aligns with your passions and your skills. The act of giving back is a deeply personal one. What genuinely resonates with you? What are you passionate about sharing with the world? By identifying your strengths and connecting them to causes you care deeply about, you'll not only inspire others, but you'll also experience a profound sense of personal fulfillment that transcends the satisfaction of personal achievement.

Remember, success isn't a solo climb; it's a shared journey. Your story has the power to illuminate the path for others, to embolden them to take risks, to overcome their fears, and to embrace their own unique potential. By sharing your wisdom, your struggles, and your triumphs, you create a ripple effect of inspiration, empowering others to chase their own dreams and, in turn, inspiring others still.

Furthermore, consider the invaluable lessons you will learn in the process of giving back. The act of explaining your journey, of articulating the challenges you overcame and the strategies you employed, forces you to examine your own experiences with a new level of clarity and depth. You will discover new facets of your own story, strengthening your understanding of your strengths and weaknesses. In essence, giving back becomes a powerful tool for self-reflection and further personal growth.

The challenges you've faced, the obstacles you've overcome
—these aren't simply elements of your past; they are powerful tools for connecting with others. They form the foundation of relatable and inspiring narratives that can help others to navigate their own struggles. Sharing these experiences, without embellishment or self-aggrandizement, creates genuine empathy and fosters deeper connections.

Don't underestimate the profound impact of simply sharing your story. The simple act of telling your journey, your successes and failures, can resonate deeply with others, offering them hope, encouragement, and a sense of community. The vulnerability inherent in sharing your imperfections humanizes your success, making it relatable and attainable for others. It transforms a seemingly unattainable feat into a possible aspiration.

Think about the power of mentorship. Mentoring is not just about imparting knowledge; it's about creating a genuine connection, fostering a trusting relationship, and providing ongoing support and guidance. By guiding others, you not only help them grow but also deepen your own understanding of your own experiences and reaffirm your own values. You strengthen your leadership skills, honing your communication and teaching abilities.

Finally, giving back is a powerful antidote to complacency. The drive to help others helps keep the fire of passion burning brightly within you. It re-energizes your commitment to continuous growth, preventing you from becoming stagnant. It reminds you of the power of your own journey and motivates you to continue pushing boundaries and inspiring those around you. The rewards are not just limited to those you help; they deeply enrich your own life.

The journey of success isn't a solitary quest; it's an interconnected web of inspiration and collaboration. By sharing your success and inspiring others to pursue their dreams, you create a positive cycle that benefits everyone involved. The summit is breathtaking, but the true beauty lies in sharing the view with others, guiding them on their own ascents, and witnessing the unfolding of their unique journeys. Embrace the opportunity to give back—it's not just about helping others; it's about enriching your own life in ways you could never have imagined. The journey continues, and it's far more rewarding when shared.

Expanding Your Definition of Achievement

The champagne bubbles have settled, the accolades have subsided, and the echo of applause fades into the quiet hum of everyday life. You've reached a summit, achieved a goal you once only dared to dream of. But as you stand on this peak, gazing out at the expansive vista before you, you might find yourself grappling with a curious sensation – a subtle unease that whispers, "Is this all there is?"

This isn't a suggestion of disappointment, but rather a natural progression. Having tasted the sweet nectar of success, you now find yourself craving a deeper, richer understanding of what success truly means. The definition you held dear—the one that propelled you through sleepless nights and unwavering dedication—might now feel... incomplete. This is perfectly normal. Our definitions of success, like our aspirations themselves, evolve and expand as we grow.

The truth is, success isn't a singular, static destination; it's a dynamic, ever-shifting landscape. The definition you embraced five years ago, ten years ago, even last year, may no longer resonate with the person you are today. Your experiences, your relationships, your understanding of the world – all these elements shape and reshape your perception of achievement. To remain stagnant in your definition is to limit your potential, to confine yourself within the boundaries of a past self.

Consider the young entrepreneur, driven by a relentless ambition to build a multi-million dollar company. For years, success was measured solely by revenue figures, market share, and the sheer volume of zeros in their bank account. They sacrificed relationships, neglected their health, and prioritized work above all else. Eventually, they achieved their financial goals, yet found themselves hollow and unfulfilled. Their definition of success had been too narrow, too focused on external validation rather than intrinsic satisfaction.

This is where the crucial shift occurs—the redefinition. It's about broadening your perspective, moving beyond the confines of materialistic or purely professional achievements. Consider the multifaceted nature of a truly fulfilling life. What about your personal relationships? The quality of time spent with loved ones? Your contributions to your community? Your physical and mental well-being? Your spiritual growth? These are all integral components of a well-rounded and successful life.

Redefining success involves a deep dive into introspection. Ask yourself: What truly brings you joy? What activities leave you feeling energized and fulfilled? What impact do you want to make on the world? The answers might surprise you. They may lead you to discover passions you never knew you possessed, goals you hadn't even considered, and a sense of purpose that transcends the conventional measures of success.

Perhaps success, for you, means nurturing your creativity through painting, writing, or composing music. Maybe it means dedicating your time to volunteer work, making a tangible difference in the lives of others. Or perhaps it's about cultivating deeper relationships, fostering meaningful connections with family and friends. The possibilities are limitless. The key is to embrace the multiplicity of your desires and aspirations, to allow yourself to define success on your own terms.

This process isn't merely about adding new elements to your definition; it's about fundamentally shifting your perspective. It's about understanding that success is not a prize to be won, but a journey to be embraced. It's about recognizing that the path to fulfillment is often winding and unpredictable, filled with unexpected detours, challenges, and moments of selfdoubt. And that's perfectly okay. In fact, it's essential.

Embrace the imperfections, the setbacks, and the lessons learned along the way. Each challenge is an opportunity for growth, each obstacle a testament to your resilience. Don't be afraid to stumble, to fall, to learn from your mistakes. It's in the process of overcoming adversity that you discover your true strength, your unwavering spirit, your capacity for resilience. These qualities, in themselves, are markers of success.

Think of a majestic oak tree, weathered by storms, scarred by lightning strikes, yet standing tall and proud. Its beauty lies not in its flawless perfection, but in its resilience, its ability to adapt and thrive despite the challenges it has faced. Your journey to success is similar. The scars you acquire along the way—the lessons you learn, the challenges you overcome—add depth, character, and beauty to your story.

This new, expanded definition of success will require you to be flexible, adaptable, and willing to constantly reassess your priorities. What may have seemed crucial a year ago might be inconsequential today. That's the nature of personal growth—it's a continuous process of evolution, learning, and re-evaluation. Embrace this fluidity, this dynamic nature of self-discovery, as a testament to your personal growth and expansion.

Remember the athlete who trains tirelessly, not just to win a single race, but to continually improve their performance, to push their physical and mental limits. Their success isn't defined by a single victory, but by the ongoing commitment to excellence, the unwavering dedication to selfimprovement. This is the essence of the ongoing journey.

Your definition of success should be a living document, a testament to your ongoing evolution. Regularly revisit your personal definition, reflecting on your progress, reassessing your priorities, and allowing your understanding of success to evolve alongside your own personal growth. This ongoing process of self-reflection and adaptation is crucial for maintaining a sense of purpose, direction, and overall wellbeing.

Consider creating a visual representation of your redefined success—a vision board, a mind map, or a journal entry detailing the various facets of a fulfilling life. Include images and descriptions that resonate with your personal aspirations, goals, and values. Make it vibrant, colorful, and representative of your unique vision of success.

This isn't just a mental exercise; it's a powerful tool for visualization and manifestation. By regularly engaging with this representation, you reinforce your commitment to your redefined success, reminding yourself of the multifaceted nature of achievement and the diverse avenues that lead to a fulfilling life.

Finally, remember that your journey is unique. Don't compare your path to others. Don't let societal expectations dictate your definition of success. Embrace your individuality, celebrate your unique strengths, and allow yourself the freedom to pursue your own path to fulfillment. Your definition of success is personal, intrinsic, and everevolving – a testament to your own unique journey of growth and discovery. The view from the summit is breathtaking, but the journey itself is an equally remarkable achievement. And that, my friends, is truly success.

Finding Fulfillment in the Process

The summit, exhilarating as it was, offers only a momentary pause. The true reward lies not just in reaching the peak, but in the unwavering commitment to the ascent itself. The journey, with its winding paths, unexpected detours, and breathtaking vistas, is where the real magic happens. It's in the relentless pursuit of self-improvement, the consistent striving for excellence, that we discover our deepest strengths and uncover a wellspring of resilience we never knew we possessed.

Think of the mountain climber, driven by an unwavering passion to conquer the peak. They don't simply focus on the summit; they immerse themselves in every aspect of the climb. They revel in the challenge of each incline, the thrill of navigating precarious terrain, the sheer satisfaction of overcoming obstacles. They find fulfillment not just in reaching the top, but in the mastery of their skills, the growth of their endurance, and the unwavering spirit that carries them forward. Their journey becomes an integral part of their identity, shaping their character and forging their spirit into something stronger, more resilient, and infinitely more fulfilling.

This is the essence of embracing the journey – finding joy and purpose not just in the destination, but in the process of becoming. It's about appreciating the small victories along the way, learning from setbacks, and celebrating the evolution of your skills and character. It's about recognizing that progress, not perfection, is the key to lasting fulfillment. We often fall prey to the allure of instant gratification, seeking quick fixes and immediate results. But true growth is a gradual unfolding, a continuous process of learning, adapting, and evolving.

Consider the artist who spends years honing their craft, meticulously refining their technique, and experimenting with new styles. They don't merely aim for a single masterpiece; they embrace the entire creative process – the sketching, the painting, the sculpting, the endless experimentation. Each brushstroke, each chisel mark, contributes to their growth as an artist. The imperfections, the failures, are all integral parts of their journey, shaping their vision and deepening their understanding of their craft. The true reward lies not in the final product, but in the transformative power of the creative process itself.

Similarly, the entrepreneur who builds a successful business doesn't simply focus on the financial rewards. They find fulfillment in the challenges of building a team, overcoming market obstacles, and innovating their products or services. Each hurdle overcome, each problem solved, strengthens their resolve and enhances their entrepreneurial skills. The journey itself, with its ups and downs, its setbacks and triumphs, becomes a source of immense personal satisfaction. The business becomes a reflection of their dedication, their resilience, and their unwavering commitment to their vision.

This principle extends beyond professional achievements. Think of the athlete who trains relentlessly, pushing their physical and mental limits. They find fulfillment not just in winning competitions, but in the process of training – the grueling workouts, the unwavering discipline, the continuous improvement of their skills. They celebrate their progress, acknowledge their setbacks, and use them as learning opportunities. Their journey becomes a testament to their perseverance, their dedication, and their unwavering commitment to self-improvement.

The key is to cultivate a mindset of continuous growth. It's about embracing the learning process, seeing challenges as opportunities for growth, and celebrating every step forward, no matter how small. It's about shifting your focus from the destination to the journey itself. Instead of solely focusing on the ultimate goal, concentrate on the daily actions that move you closer to it. Break down large, daunting objectives into smaller, manageable steps. Celebrate each milestone achieved, however insignificant it might seem.

Cultivate a sense of gratitude for the experiences, both positive and negative, that shape your journey. Each challenge you overcome, each setback you endure, adds to your resilience and strengthens your character. Learn to see setbacks not as failures, but as valuable lessons that contribute to your growth. Embrace the imperfections, for they are the building blocks of your progress. Remember that the journey is not linear; it's a winding path with unexpected twists and turns. Embrace the uncertainty, for it's in the unexpected detours that we often discover new opportunities and unexpected joys.

To truly embrace the journey, you need to cultivate selfcompassion. Be kind to yourself, acknowledge your limitations, and forgive yourself for mistakes. Avoid comparing your journey to others. Each person's path is unique, reflecting their individual circumstances, skills, and aspirations. Comparing yourself to others only serves to undermine your confidence and discourage your progress. Celebrate your own achievements, no matter how small. Acknowledge your progress, and be grateful for the journey you're on.

Visualize your future self, the person you aspire to become. Imagine the skills you will acquire, the challenges you will overcome, and the person you will evolve into through this journey. Allow this vision to inspire and motivate you. Let it fuel your commitment to continuous growth and propel you forward on your path to fulfillment.

Incorporate mindfulness into your daily life. Take time each day to appreciate the present moment, to savor the small joys, and to reflect on your progress. Practice gratitude for the opportunities and experiences that come your way. Mindfulness helps you to stay present, to appreciate the journey, and to avoid getting caught up in the anxiety of the future.

The journey of personal growth is a marathon, not a sprint. It's a continuous process of learning, evolving, and adapting. Embrace the challenges, celebrate the victories, and never stop learning. Remember that the greatest reward is not the destination, but the transformation you undergo along the way. The skills you acquire, the resilience you develop, and the person you become—these are the true treasures of the journey. So, embrace the process, find joy in the present moment, and revel in the remarkable transformation that awaits you.

The path to your dreams is paved not just with accomplishments, but with the experiences, the lessons, the growth that comes from the continuous striving. It is a tapestry woven with threads of resilience, perseverance, and an unwavering belief in your own potential. Embrace the imperfections, the detours, the moments of doubt; they are all part of the vibrant, unique story of your journey. Don't just reach the destination; savor the incredible, transformative adventure that gets you there. For in the journey, in the continuous growth, lies the true and lasting fulfillment. And that, my friends, is a reward far greater than any summit you could ever reach. The summit is a milestone, a testament to your dedication, but the journey itself is the masterpiece you've created. It is the story you are writing, and it is a story worth celebrating, every single chapter, every single word. So, continue writing your story, one step, one experience, one triumph at a time. And know that the journey itself is the greatest accomplishment of all. This journey, your journey, is a testament to your strength, your spirit, and your unwavering pursuit of a life lived with passion, purpose, and unyielding joy. Embrace it. Live it.
Love it. And never, ever stop.

Acknowledgments

First and foremost, I want to express my deepest gratitude to my family and friends for their unwavering support and encouragement throughout the writing process. Their belief in me fueled my perseverance, even during the most challenging moments. A special thanks goes to [Name of specific person and their contribution, e.g., my editor, Jane Doe, for her insightful feedback and tireless dedication]. Her expertise and guidance were invaluable in shaping this book into its final form. I'm also indebted to [Name of another person and their contribution, e.g., my writing group, The Scribblers, for their constructive criticism and unwavering enthusiasm]. Their support provided a much-needed creative spark. Finally, thank you to every reader who picks up this book. Your journey to achieving your dreams inspires me, and I hope this book empowers you to continue on that path.

Appendix

This appendix contains additional resources to support your journey:

Worksheet 1: Identifying Your Passions: A printable worksheet to guide you through the process of uncovering your deepest desires.
Worksheet 2: SMART Goal Setting: A template to help you define specific, measurable, achievable, relevant, and time-bound goals.
Worksheet 3: Overcoming Limiting Beliefs: Exercises to help you identify and reframe negative self-talk. **Resource List:** A curated list of books, websites, and organizations

offering further support in personal development and goal achievement. (Links to be provided in the online version).

Glossary

SMART Goals: Specific, Measurable, Achievable, Relevant, and Time-bound goals.
Limiting Beliefs: Negative thoughts or assumptions that hinder personal growth and achievement.
Resilience: The ability to bounce back from setbacks and adversity.
Mindfulness: The practice of paying attention to the present moment without judgment.
Self-Compassion: Treating oneself with kindness, understanding, and acceptance.

References

References
Brown, B. (2012). Daring greatly: How the courage to be vulnerable transforms the way we live, love, parent, and lead. Gotham Books.

Brown, B. (2010). The gifts of imperfection: Let go of who you think you're supposed to be and embrace who you are. Hazelden Publishing.

Coelho, P. (1988). The Alchemist. HarperOne. Harris, R. (2008). The happiness trap: How to stop struggling and start living. Shambhala Publications. Holler, J. (2019). Fear is my homeboy: How to slay doubt, boss up, and succeed on your own terms.
Greenleaf Book Group Press.

Jeffers, S. (2007). Feel the fear and do it anyway. Ballantine Books.

Kahneman, D. (2011). Thinking, fast and slow. Farrar, Straus and Giroux.

Latham, G. P., & Locke, E. A. (2007). New developments in and directions for goal-setting research. European Psychologist, 12(4), 290-300. Locke, E. A., & Latham, G. P. (2002). Building a practically useful theory of goal setting and task motivation: A 35-year odyssey. American Psychologist, 57(9), 705-717.

Locke, E. A., & Latham, G. P. (2006). New directions in goal-setting theory. Current Directions in Psychological Science, 15(5), 265-268.

Morisano, D., Hirsh, J. B., Peterson, J. B., Pihl, R. O., & Shore, B. M. (2010). Setting, elaborating, and reflecting on personal goals improves academic performance. Journal of Applied Psychology, 95(2), 255-264.

Schwartz, D. J. (1959). The magic of thinking big.

Simon & Schuster.

Weinberg, R. S., & Gould, D. (2018). Foundations of sport and exercise psychology (7th ed.). Human Kinetics.

This bibliography includes a mix of classic self-help books, academic studies on goal-setting and motivation, and contemporary works on overcoming fear and building confidence. These sources could provide a strong foundation for the themes likely to be explored in "I Dream, I Dare, I Do"

The inclusion of academic sources like Locke & Latham's work on goal-setting theory and Morisano et al.'s study on personal goals and academic performance adds scientific credibility to the self-help concepts. Meanwhile, popular self-help books like "Feel the Fear and Do It Anyway" and "The Magic of Thinking Big" align with the motivational and confidence-building aspects of the book. Works by Brené Brown on vulnerability and imperfection contribute to the "Dare" aspect of the book's title, offering insights on overcoming self-doubt and embracing one's true self . The inclusion of "The Alchemist" by Paulo Coelho, while not a traditional selfhelp book, provides a narrative perspective on following one's dreams, which could be referenced as an inspirational story within the book.

This bibliography provides a balanced mix of popular self-help literature and academic research, which could be used to support the ideas and strategies presented in "I Dream, I Dare, I Do". It offers readers the opportunity to delve deeper into the topics of goalsetting, motivation, and personal development, enhancing the book's value as a comprehensive guide to pursuing one's dreams and overcoming obstacles.

Author Biography

Christy Moore Winborn is a motivational speaker, life coach, and fiction writer with a passion for helping others unlock their full potential. She has over 20 years of experience in relationship, life, business development coaching, and corporate training and has witnessed firsthand the transformative power of self-belief and consistent action. Christy's engaging writing style combines practical advice with inspirational storytelling, making complex concepts accessible and relatable to a wide audience. Beyond their professional pursuits, Christy enjoys writing, designing, and enjoying her family.

You can connect with Christy on LinkedIn:
   https://www.linkedin.com/in/christymoorewinborn/